A COLLECTION
OF STORIES

Robert C. Gwin, III

Visit our website at **www.StillwaterPress.com** for more information.

First Stillwater River Publications Edition

Library of Congress Control Number: 2019920860

ISBN: 978-1-950339-67-9

1 2 3 4 5 6 7 8 9 10
Written by Robert C. Gwin, III.
Published by Stillwater River Publications, Pawtucket, RI, USA.

A Collection of Stories

TABLE OF CONTENTS

AN INTRODUCTION

In his 1966 novel *Satori in Paris*, Jack Kerouac wrote the following: "…made-up stories and romances about what would happen IF are for children and adult cretins who are afraid to read themselves in a book…"

This bothered me when I read it both because I have always enjoyed and respected Kerouac's writing, and because much of my writing hangs on an IF. It was only then I realized that stories asking how people might react IF can allow us to ask "What would I do IF?" and thereby read ourselves in a book.

This collection begins by asking "What If?"

WHAT IF?

What if a little girl set out with a basket of goodies to visit her grandmother and she came upon a wolf? What if a boy traded his cow for some magic beans and grew a gigantic beanstalk? What if a besieging army built a large hollow wooden horse? What if a man built a submarine that could go 20,000 leagues under the sea? What if a young medical student assembled a body out of cadaver pieces and was able to give it life? What if two teenagers put together an elaborate plan to escape from their feuding families and run away and it went horribly wrong? What if a scientist developed a potion that made him invisible? What if a little girl fell down a rabbit hole into a magical land? What if an intelligent computer decided to take over a spaceship? What if an astronaut, thought to be dead, was abandoned on Mars? What if a teenage girl lived with seven dwarves? What if an adopted orphan suddenly discovered her magical fairy godmother? What if a man was told to take his son to the top of a mountain and sacrifice him to God? What if a man leading his people to a new land was able to part the sea so they could escape? What if a young boy with only a slingshot volunteered to fight a giant clad in armor? What if a warrior leading his men home from battle encountered a giant

Cyclops? What if a strange count was forced to live on the blood of young women? What if a man decided to tell the world that the Martians were invading, and they believed him? What if a general coming home from war was met by three witches who told him he would become the king? What if a young prince of Denmark was told to avenge the murder of his father who had been killed by his uncle? What if an old man were to catch a giant marlin only to have the sharks devour it before he reached shore? What if a couple were told they could have any fruit in the orchard except an apple and they ate the apple anyway? What if books were illegal and a fireman's job was to burn them? What if a man invented a time machine and travelled thousands of years into the future? What if the animals killed the farmer and set up a socialist farm? What if there were three laws of robotics? What if, told that her disgraced brother must remain unburied, a girl risked death to bury him? What if a middle-aged man, infatuated with young girls, moved in with and then married the mother of a particularly seductive nymphet? What if an uneducated boy and a runaway slave took off on a raft down the Mississippi River? What if a one-legged whaling ship captain went on a crazed search for the great white whale that had injured him? What if a miserly businessman was visited by three spirits on Christmas Eve? What if?

MRS. TAFFETA'S GIFT SHOP

Mrs. Taffeta's gift shop occupied the entire first floor of a beautifully restored large Victorian home in Westfield, Massachusetts. The outside colors combined the classic dusty pinks, light blues, and white accents that so characterized the Romantic style. Virginia Taffeta lived on the second and third floors, both of which were well-furnished with period antiques.

The gift shop contained a range of practical and whimsical items, ranging from embroidered tea towels to odd kitchen tools to beautiful silk scarfs. There were, of course, scented candles of many sizes and a small book section containing books by local authors, books about the sights to be seen in that area of Massachusetts, and a few specialized cookbooks. In the corner, seated behind a large, beautifully finished oak desk sat "Mrs." Taffeta, who in fact was not married and had no plans ever to be so encumbered. She had chosen "Mrs. Taffeta's" instead of "Miss Taffeta's" because it was felt that "Miss" brought up visions of a cold lonely spinster, whereas "Mrs." reminded you of your mother or grandmother and would make most people feel warm and snuggly.

There were, along the backside of the building, at the seam

between the first and second floors, three brass hinges which allowed one to open up the building and rearrange things in Mrs. Taffeta's gift shop, for, you see, the entire building was an elaborate dollhouse built for his granddaughter, Dorothy, by Hiram Wentworth. It had been Dorothy herself who, only nine at the time, had decided that the first floor should be named and decorated as "Mrs. Taffeta's Gift Shop." And it was Dorothy who chose "Mrs." instead of "Miss." Together with her grandfather she had found, or made, all the tiny gift items in the shop. Dorothy enjoyed rearranging and redecorating as the seasons passed, making sure that Mrs. Taffeta always had merchandise appropriate for the next holiday.

Grandpa Wentworth often dropped by the house to see how things were going at the gift shop and Dorothy would tell him the latest news.

"Grandpa, you won't believe it. There was a robbery."

"A robbery? I hope no one was hurt."

"Oh, it wasn't that kind of a robbery. It was Timmy Whitehead. He stole a little scarf to give to Melody Blaine for her birthday."

"Why did he steal it?"

"He was too shy to let anyone know he liked Melody and he knew Mrs. Taffeta would ask who the scarf was for, so he just snuck out the door. Of course Mrs. Taffeta saw the whole thing."

"Well, what happened? Did Mrs. Taffeta call the police?"

"Oh no, Grandpa. You don't know Mrs. Taffeta very well. She wrote a very nice note to Timmy's mother. 'Dear Mrs. Whitehead,' it said. 'I was so pleased to see Timmy in my shop yesterday. He certainly is growing up fast. He picked out the prettiest little silk scarf. I think it will be a present for that adorable little Blaine girl he seems to be so fond of. I was all ready to put the scarf in a little box and gift wrap it when Timmy just walked out the door. I think he was a little shy about buying a present for a girl. I'd still be glad to giftwrap it for him if he would like to come by. He could bring the ten dollars to pay for the scarf at the same time. Yours truly, Virginia Taffeta.'"

"That Mrs. Taffeta is certainly a sweetie. So, what happened?"

"Well Timmy didn't come back, but his mother came by the shop the next day, full of apologies, and paid Mrs. Taffeta her ten dollars. I hope she let Timmy give the scarf to Melody."

I remember my mother telling me that story when I was not much older than she had been at the time. Just looking at this old dollhouse brings it all back. I can't believe I am dusting it off for my own granddaughter.

MAGIC

The nine-year-old and the seven-year-old had been making Fairy Houses in the back yard in the corner under the big shade tree. The nine-year-old decided she had had enough and went inside to read her book, leaving her sister alone with the Fairy Village they had created. As soon as she was alone the seven-year-old realized that what she had always thought of as an odd bit of sunlight was actually The Magic. When she realized it, her first reaction was to tell her sister, but that idea quickly vanished. Why tell her?

She tried to remember everything she could about people using The Magic. Most of what she could recall came from stories about evil witches turning handsome princes into ugly frogs. Well, she didn't know any handsome princes, she didn't much like frogs, and she didn't want to be an evil witch. How about that pesky wasp? Wouldn't he be much nicer as a pretty butterfly? And so it was. No abracadabra or magic wands, just a feeling that things should be that way. This wasn't hard. You just needed to be able to see The Magic, know what it was, and then use it. Ah, but could she take it with her, or did it just work when she was in the Fairy Village? She walked across the yard, found a worm, and turned him into a blue bird. Okay, this was getting more interesting every moment. And just then her mother announced dinner. Too bad, she sighed. Oh well, perhaps she could find it again tomorrow.

And then her Brussels sprouts turned into green beans, much to her sister's distress. "How come she gets green beans and I get sprouts?"

"Oh, I guess Papa found some of the beans from last night and gave them to your sister. Those sprouts won't kill you." And before Papa could come in from the kitchen, he got an important phone call that lasted all through dinner. So she could take The Magic with her, at least for a while.

The seven-year-old was smart enough and had already read enough to know that Magic could be big trouble. Apprentices were forever setting off disasters which only the real magician could fix. But she was the only magician around, so she needed to be very careful. No big Magics, such as a new truck for Papa or a new car for Mama. And even turning her sister's hair green was probably not a great idea. But what could she do while she had this power? Something good but not too dramatic. She found that when it was her turn to pick up all the toys in the playroom, and no one else was in that part of the house, a little magic went a long way. And she learned that picking everything up and putting it in its place in less than a minute caused her older sister to get very suspicious. No one complained when the tomato plants and the green bean plants produced exceptional crops. In fact, she soon realized, her mama and papa just assumed it was a result of their excellent care. And at seven she learned an important lesson; when at all possible, people want to assume that good results are due to their own hard work. This was especially the case with her older sister who returned from the shooting range after a full session during which she hit all bull's-eyes.

It was the blueberry bushes that were her undoing. By the end of the summer there were no more blueberries and she wondered if, perhaps, it might be possible for them to have a second crop. She asked both Mama and Papa if she might try giving the bushes some plant food and lots of water. They both assured her that the blueberry season was over, but that if she wanted to feed and water the blueberry plants maybe that would produce more berries next year, and it certainly wouldn't hurt anything. And so she set out, knowing that plant food and water were only a cover for what she was really planning. She didn't notice that her sister was paying very close attention.

Two weeks later, much to everyone's surprise, the blueberry bushes started blossoming and then only a few days after that, berries started to appear. Her parents weren't paying much attention, so they didn't notice when blueberries the size of grapes were starting to cover the bushes. The seven-year-old picked them as fast as she could and looked all over for places to hide them. By the end of the week the blueberries were the size of apricots and they were growing as fast as she could pull them off the bushes. It was when the berries grew to the size of oranges and started to break the branches that her older sister pulled her into their room and said, "This has gone too far and I am going to stop it right now before we get buried in blue watermelons." She then went out the door, walked directly to the Fairy Houses, and kicked them apart, scattering the pieces in all directions. The light disappeared and so did The Magic. The blueberry bushes were suddenly as they should be at the end of the summer and all the giant-sized fruit that had begun to accumulate under them was gone. The seven-year-old walked slowly to her big sister, took her hand and said softly, "Thank you."

PRINCESS GWENDOLYN

G wendolyn awoke uncommonly early, for her, on that sunny summer day. She slowly realized that the maid had not yet brought her morning cup of hot chocolate or her dish of fresh sliced fruit. She lay in her large soft bed and began to drum her fingers on the pink duvet that covered her.

Time passed and still no maid. It was long after sunrise. Gwendolyn contemplated the, unusual for her, idea of getting out of her snuggly bed even before the maid arrived to help dress her. She could not recall a morning in which she had dressed herself. She was now sixteen years old and had recently read in her *Pretty Princesses* magazine that girls (princesses of course) were now expected to dress themselves as early as age ten. When she had read this she dismissed the whole idea as a preposterous pipedream. But this morning, with still no maid in sight, Gwendolyn began to ponder the imponderable: getting out of her warm bed and dressing herself with no maid, no chocolate, and no fresh fruit.

But, oh dear, poor Gwendolyn had no idea where her clothes were kept. They seemed to arrive with the maid and the chocolate and the fresh fruit. But how could the maid carry chocolate, fresh fruit, and clothes? Even to Gwendolyn's only lightly exercised mind that made no sense.

In spite of everything that argued against it, Gwendolyn lifted the sheet and duvet and lay uncovered. She slowly sat up and swung her legs off the bed with her feet now only inches from the floor. Her heart was beating with uncommon rapidity and she had a strong urge to fall back onto her warm pillows, pull up the bedclothes, and wait for the maid no matter how long that took. But Gwendolyn reminded herself that even in this difficult situation she was, after all, a real princess.

With her mouth clenched and an expression of grim determination on her face, Gwendolyn lowered her feet to the floor, stood up, and took a step away from her bed. She felt very proud of herself. And then across the room she saw the large armoire. Could that be where her clothes were kept? Gwendolyn slowly and carefully crossed the room until she faced two large doors. Much to her dismay the doors were closed. She searched in her memory to find how the maid had opened these doors and recalled that those two brass handles might be the answer. Gwendolyn firmly grasped one handle and slowly pulled the door open. Then she did the same with the other door. Before her were arranged all her beautiful clothes.

And then Gwendolyn heard a soft buzzing sound which seemed to get louder and louder and would not stop and suddenly Rebecca awoke from her beautiful dream to the darkness of a cold January morning. She pounded the alarm clock until it stopped making all that noise.

She was no longer a princess and knew she hadn't been since the arrival of her little sister Jessica. She was just Rebecca Stone and she had to get dressed, get downstairs, eat some breakfast, make a lunch, load up her backpack, and get out the front door in time to catch the school bus. And never a maid to help her.

THE STRANGE TALE
OF BANJO THE CLOWN

B anjo the Circus Clown, at sixty-five, knew he was getting old. Everyone gets older but he was getting old. His tired fingers had begun to shake as he fashioned balloon animals for the children and recently, he had been fighting the urge to slap some of the more obnoxious little brats.

It was on a sunny Wednesday that Death came for Banjo. Banjo knew he was getting old but this was much too soon. He pleaded with Death, "Oh sir, I believe you have made a mistake. You are probably looking for Blimpo the Clown, or perhaps Boingo, with whom I am often confused. And, just for you, here is a balloon monkey, one of my most difficult creations."

Death was quite used to resistance and claims that there must be some mistake, but in all eternity no one had ever offered him a balloon monkey. He pondered the situation and then, with a very suspicious smile, responded. "WELL, PERHAPS YOU ARE CORRECT. THE THREE NAMES ARE VERY SIMILAR AND YOU ARE ALL CLOWNS. IT IS POSSIBLE THAT A MISTAKE HAS BEEN MADE. THANK YOU VERY MUCH FOR THE MONKEY." Death and the monkey vanished.

Banjo did not know what to think. How long was his reprieve? A few days, a few weeks, even years? Had there really been a mistake? Feeling quite happy Banjo went back to making balloons and vowed not to slap anyone. Had he been aware of Death's rather strange sense of humor, however, he would not have been as happy.

The first example of Death's idea of fun was the strange demise of Blimpo. Although he had been scheduled to live another twenty years, he met an early end in a bizarre accident. Blimpo had fallen asleep in the clown car one night and, for reasons never explained, the car was towed early the next morning to the junk yard with Blimpo still asleep inside and immediately crushed. It was only his red wig and clown shoes which somehow stuck out of the flattened vehicle that alerted the junkyard boss that something might be wrong. Poor Blimpo!

Boingo's end, only a few days later, occurred one morning as the "Flying Hootchies" were rehearsing new trapeze tricks. Boingo, who was infatuated by Carmelita, the youngest and sexiest of the troupe, was standing just inside the center ring. With his attention totally concentrated on Carmelita far above, he leaned back and fell over the ring border right into the path of the elephants having their morning run around the big top. He ended almost as flat as Blimpo. Had he been able to tell anyone, Boingo would have said that he felt a slight push just as he fell back. Poor Boingo!

Death had saved his most amusing — to him anyway — trick for Banjo. First, he made Banjo's body twenty years younger and then he made him immortal. Some joke!

Banjo awoke the next morning feeling wonderful. Nothing ached. His clothes didn't seem to fit though. They were too big around the waist and too tight across his chest and his pant legs

14

were too short. He had more hair on his head and instead of gray it was brown. At breakfast he ate twice as much as usual and instead of feeling like an after-breakfast nap he went for a long walk and even found himself jogging a little.

The entire circus was still recovering from the sudden deaths of Blimpo and Boingo, but it never occurred to Banjo that he might be responsible. One afternoon as they all prepared for the matinee, Banjo felt an emotion he had not experienced for many years. When the Teenage Tumbling Texans went by dressed in their skintight costumes Banjo felt lust. And it felt good.

Months went by and people remarked on how good Banjo looked and asked for his secret. He only smiled, shrugged his shoulders, and said, "Just lucky I guess." Some luck!

It took a full year before Banjo admitted to himself that something very strange was happening. Not only did he look and feel young, but he seemed accident proof. Normal circus accidents, such as pieces of apparatus falling from high places, never hit him. Things fell in front, behind, to the left, and to the right, but never on Banjo. The knife thrower got angry with his wife one night and started throwing knives at her. Two came out the door of their trailer as Banjo was walking by and both seemed to just curve around him.

Five years had gone by with no sign of aging and even his friends were starting to avoid him. Banjo had already accepted the fact that he wasn't going to die in an accident. He considered trying a self-inflicted wound, but he didn't want to kill himself just to find out that he could die. He became the head clown both because he was the oldest and because he had the energy to think up and work out new clown routines.

Ten years had gone by and Banjo was seventy-five years

old, but his body was still the same as when he was forty-five. He was still attracted to women and at first, they were attracted to him, but eventually his real age was revealed (perhaps by a rival suitor) and the women wanted nothing to do with him. By this time many of his friends had left the circus and it appeared that the days of the traveling circus were over. And then the circus closed. Banjo was well passed retirement age, but his young body was eager to start a new career. In spite of age discrimination laws, absolutely no one wanted to hire a seventy-five-year-old circus clown even if he looked and acted forty-five. He had saved a little money and received a modest Social Security check, so he had a place to live and food to eat.

When Banjo reached ninety-five, still in his forty-five-year-old body, he was called into the motor vehicle department for an examination to see if he was still fit to drive. Of course he passed all the tests, but the inspectors felt there was something odd about his claim to be ninety-five years old. The next thing Banjo knew, he received a letter from the Social Security Administration asking him to report to the local office for a review of his status. Banjo realized that not only would they probably cut off his Social Security payments, but they would probably have him arrested for falsely collecting all these years and he'd be sent to prison.

As Banjo stood on the sidewalk across from the Social Security office, waiting for the cross-town bus to pass, Death, deciding that enough was enough, took pity on Banjo and threw him under the bus.

OUR PRINCESS

Disgusted by the corruption sweeping the land, Our Princess took her gold-plated shotgun and with a fiendish gleam in her eyes shot The Devil and The Devil's silver cow. Of course, shooting The Devil is ultimately a waste of time since he'll be back within a few months, a year at the most. The silver cow is another situation entirely. Although it looks to be a normal barn animal that has been spray-painted silver, that cow is, in fact, The Devil's luggage. It is full of all sorts of tricks and nastiness, plus, of course, a few changes of under-wear and a clean shirt. So the question always arises: what to do with a dead cow that contains devilish things? Having done this a few times already Our Princess had come up with a novel approach which, she felt, would at least slow The Devil down as he tried to reconstitute his cow and find that clean shirt.

In the past Our Princess had tried burning the cow whole over a large bonfire. To the surprise of us all, the cow simply started to expand until it was the size of a hot air balloon and then lifted up and floated away into the night sky. Clearly that was not the way to rid the world of the bedeviled bovine. The next time she tried a case of dynamite shoved down its throat. We were picking hamburger and clean socks out of the treetops for weeks. Like idiots we put all the bits into one large pile, which, when it reached a certain percentage of the whole, reconstituted itself, shook its tail, and "poof" disappeared to wherever The Devil's cow grazes. The Princess did save a large black sock which once could be seen in the royal museum.

This time Our Princess ordered many flasks of liquid nitrogen with which she froze the dead silver cow. Then she wrapped it in a large thin mesh net and dropped it from a high tower. Of course, it shattered into hundreds of pieces. Before they could thaw Our Princess placed each piece in a waterproof container and Fed-Ex'd each one to a different country. Go find your clean shirt now Mr. Devil.

Unfortunately, getting rid of The Devil and his silver cow did not end the corruption. Our Princess's father, Good King Wassisname, was, let's face it, a doddering old fool. The kingdom was being run by the "King's Chamber Council," a group of noblemen elected by the ten percent of the population who bothered to vote in the "free and independent" elections. Of course, the Chamber Council ran the country in such a way as to benefit themselves. When they needed a fancier vacation destination, they increased taxes and blamed the cost of retirees' health insurance. The population cursed the retirees and paid up. The fact that there were no retirees with health insurance was never brought up. When the local newspaper tried to get a list of retirees it was refused on the grounds of "professional privacy." The paper gave up without asking what the heck was "professional privacy." The Chamber Council then took out a large, expensive advertisement praising the paper's continual concern for the role of a free press in society. So much for investigative reporting.

Our Princess was getting fed up with the entire situation.

Getting rid of The Devil had not helped, and trying to get people to come out and elect a new, less corrupt Chamber Council resulted only in the members of the Chamber Council being re-elected with more votes than usual, since no one else wanted the job.

The fiendish gleam was blazing from both eyes on the day that Our Princess brought fiscal responsibility to our fair land and ended corruption for all time. The first thing she did was to load her gold-plated shotgun and shoot her father, the useless old king. Then she declared herself Queen, shot the members of the Chamber Council, and installed a new council of people who had no desire to go on expensive vacations. And it must be admitted, having seen what happened to the last council, had no desire to rule the land for their own benefit. [Lest there be any confusion I must note here that although she is officially the Queen, she will always be Our Princess.]

When The Devil had finally gathered up everything but that one sock he returned to our fair land and, having retrieved his missing laundry, surveyed our now peaceful and completely uncorrupt land. As he and his reconstituted cow slowly faded from view, we heard him sigh, "Oh pooh, this place is no fun anymore."

A PIRATE

"'Ah!' I hear you say. 'What kind of a pirate are you? You with no peg leg or hook for a hand or even a pet parrot.' Well, lady, those are not the important things. I do have this fine pirate ship and my crew of hearty sailors, and, the most important of all, I know where the real treasure is. And you say, 'You know where the treasure is buried?' And I say, 'Did I say it was buried? Who said it was buried?' And then you say, 'Well, wherever it is, why don't you just go get it and split it up with your hearty mates and give up this desperate life of high seas piracy?'

"Well, there are a number of things you haven't considered. First, maybe I know where the treasure is but it isn't that easy to retrieve. Or, perhaps it would be easy but the cost is too high. Maybe I would have to crush kittens. Or—and I'm sure that you have never considered this possibility—maybe I just enjoy being a pirate. Arrrggggga!"

And with that statement to the little old lady in pale blue standing at the dockside, we cast off the bow line, cast off the stern, and on the main jib alone, headed out into the channel on our way to more fame and possible fortune, and nice looking babes as we continued to rampage up and down the coast of

20

Cape Cod. It was summer and all the tourists from the Midwest had arrived to see the sea. "Look, Mildred, that's the Atlantic Ocean. Do you want to go on a whale watch this afternoon?" We were due into P Town for the afternoon "Ride with a real pirate" excursion, for which the Chamber of Commerce got thirty dollars a head and only gave us twenty-five. And since that drunk from Attleboro fell overboard last year, they limited us to thirty passengers and made them all wear lifejackets. We found it was rather surprising that most of the tourists like wearing the jackets, especially when we told them that we all had to look out for rogue waves which could come out of nowhere and tip the boat over. It was exciting and they were all relieved to return to the dock without being carried down to Davy Jones' locker. We were cautioned by the chamber not to be too helpful putting life jackets on the young ladies. We are a hearty crew!

Well, on this particular voyage "we was loaded to the gunnels" — we had all thirty passengers — and the cargo was looking good. We had a bachelorette party from Boston who had already done the wine tasting tour in Hyannis, Falmouth, and North Truro and were ready to party on. A few of them really needed assistance from the younger members of our crew in correctly donning their lifejackets. A good time was being had by all, except for Mildred from Iowa. She started heaving as soon as we left the dock. We rounded the tip of Long Point and headed for Wood End Light. We would then cruise past Herring Cove Beach before heading out into the open ocean. The seas were calm but there was a nice breeze out of the northeast, and we were making good time. Some of the crew were trying a bit too hard, but there were no complaints. I had alerted everyone to start looking for whales as well as rogue waves when First Mate One-Eyed Pete suddenly declared "Mutiny!" We explained to the passengers that they would have to decide if they wanted to join Pete and his men—two fine looking young men—or have snacks with me—I am the captain—and a guy from the Chamber of Commerce. Mildred stopped barfing long enough to start screaming that they were all going to die, but the bachelorettes all went off with Pete and his mutineers. We heard happy sounds from below. They must have decided to continue the wine tour. We broke out the standard refreshments. Milk, bottled water, and cookies for Mildred and those who had remained on deck. The wind had dropped, and we were moving slowly when Pete appeared on deck and said he thought that since we weren't going anywhere it should be swim time. We hove to, dropped sail, deployed the swimming ladders, and watched the younger folks leap overboard. They were required to keep their life vests on, but several were naughty children. Pete and his crew are all certified lifeguards and they were closely attending their charges. The guy from the Chamber of Commerce could only ask, "Does this happen all the time?" My response was simply, "Only in the mating season."

The youngsters, most of them now sober, climbed up the ladders and dry towels appeared for each wet body. When all were present and accounted for, we raised sail and turned south back towards land. We saw no whales or rogue waves on that trip, but everyone, including Mildred, agreed it had been an excellent high seas adventure.

And in case you haven't realized it, days like these are the real pirate treasure.

HAPPY BIRTHDAY GRANDPA

The car trip from the city had been difficult for my grandfather. He was not used to being away from the nursing home and its staff of attentive caregivers. The motion of the car and the noise of the highway had confused him. He would occasionally drift off to sleep only to wake up, look uncertainly around, and be unable to vocalize the confusion that he felt. He was no longer the robust athletic man I remembered from when I was a teenager. The few wisps of white hair that remained on his otherwise bald head and the frail, slightly shrunken body were almost an insult to my memories of him. When we finally left the main highway and slowly moved along a quieter country road, my grandfather seemed to finally become aware of the world outside the car. "Am I going home?" he asked with wonder in his voice.

"No, Grandpa, you are going on a birthday expedition. Today you are ninety-five years old and we are going to visit a place none of has seen for many years. Do you remember your old summer camp? It's still there, even though no one camps there anymore. The son of your old handyman John Rockwell runs by every few months just to make sure there are no problems."

A few minutes later the car turned off the paved road onto a dirt and gravel lane that led into the woods. Grandfather was now very attentively looking from one side of the car to the other. The woods were thick for the first couple of miles until suddenly they gave way to a beautiful wide-open valley, at the center of which was a small cabin with a porch facing east. The car rolled up to the structure and stopped. "That's my cabin. And my chair is still on the porch." His voice seemed stronger now, almost assured, as the familiarity of his surroundings overcame the confusion of the car and highway. My wife and I helped him out of the car and let him just look at the vista before him. We got him up onto the porch and, with slow shuffling steps, he led us to his chair and settled into it. "It feels a bit stiff."

"Grandpa, it is brand new, from LL's. Happy birthday." I sat on the porch and looked out on a scene I had viewed every summer from the time I was five until I graduated from high school.

Looking toward the east, the blazing sun illuminated a gorgeous field rising from a fringe of beautiful trees, a mix of pines and elms (Grandpa had often said there had been more elms prior to the 1938 hurricane). I could remember the smell of the various growth of flowers and foliage; lily of the valley, lilac, goldenrod, daisies, each dependent upon a particular season.

Gazing north, one could see the glorious maple trees which were tapped and would be running sap in early spring. The sap then had to be carried (and, according to Grandpa, sampled along the way) before boiling to reduce the residue to very tasty maple syrup. I can still taste it.

We sat there taking in the scene and remembering past years. "Where is Mathew?" my grandfather asked. Mathew, my father, had died the previous year.

"Oh, as usual, he just can't get away from his work. He did send his best wishes for your birthday."

"That boy always did work too hard. He's a good boy."

We sat quietly for almost an hour, both of us remembering lost years, when my grandfather turned to me and said, "Maybe we should start back now, Timmy." I was slightly surprised that he had even remembered my name, and even more surprised that he seemed to understand where he was and where we had come from that morning. We returned, slowly, to the car, and started the long drive back to the city.

That was last time Grandpa saw the cabin. He died that winter. It's a long drive from Connecticut to that part of Maine and now that the kids are getting older, a stop at The Desert of Maine is no longer a treat, and they would rather shop online than actually go into the LL Beans store in Freeport. I have thought about selling the property, but the remembrance of the glorious maple trees and the lily of the valley, lilac, gold-enrod, and daisies, each dependent upon a particular season, has prevented me from letting it go. Perhaps my children will enjoy it one day. Happy birthday Grandpa!

THE MYSTERY OF THE
VERMONT SYRUP SUCKER

My name is Sally Ann Cruthers and I am ten years old. I like to be a detective and solve mysteries. My big brother, he is twelve, is usually no help at all, but on this occasion, he provided the answer. I call this case "The Mystery of the Vermont Syrup Sucker."

We used to live in Manhattan, that's New York City, in a big apartment. Both our parents worked long hours and were big shots in whatever it was that they did. My brother and I had a series of nannies. I could tell you about some of them, but not here. The nanny would get us up in the morning, get us off to school, pick us up after school, make sure we did our homework, feed us dinner, and get us into bed. We were usually asleep by the time our parents got home. On the weekends, anyway, the whole family did stuff together and that was fun. There's lots to do in New York, and in the winter sometimes we would go skiing in Vermont. That was really fun.

So, one day my father announces that we are moving to Vermont to live in a cheese factory. Well, it used to be a place where they made cheese, but now it was a great big house. The place where my parents worked had been bought by some other company and now neither of them had to go to work anymore. They had to do stuff on their computers sometimes, but now they would be home all the time.

The people in Vermont move and talk a lot slower than the people in New York. It takes a while to get used to it, but I like it much better. It's friendlier. And, no more nannies!

Our neighbor, Mr. Johnson, is a maple syrup farmer. Being from the city, and knowing that maple syrup comes from trees, I guess I thought you hooked the little bottles up to a tree branch and filled it up with syrup. Mr. Johnson showed me and my brother how it's really done. As soon as winter even begins to lessen, you go out in the woods and pound little tube things into the trees, and then hook them up to about a million miles of plastic tubing. Every now and then there is a collection barrel that the sap from a whole bunch of trees runs into. Of course, I thought the sap was maple syrup. Of course, I was wrong. You have to gather up all the sap and take it to the boiling house and you boil it. And it turns into maple syrup. I don't know how that happens. And you get a whole lot less syrup than the amount of sap you started with. Once it has turned into syrup, you pour it into big containers, and they go into the storage room. And that is where this mystery begins. Mr. Johnson told me that strange creatures called the Vermont Syrup Suckers sometimes sneak into the storage room and suck the sap right out of the containers. No one has ever caught one or even taken a picture of one, because except for its eyes it is invisible. I thought it was a joke, but Mr. Johnson said they are real, and they always stole the syrup while it was still warm, and only at night. After the containers cooled, there was always a little bit less syrup than when they were warm. I even asked some of the other men who worked with Mr. Johnson if there was less syrup when the containers were cool, and they all said that it often happens. Right then I determined to investigate because I was sure Mr. Johnson was making fun of me and the fact that I was a city girl.

I decided that I would spend the night in the container room after a new batch of warm syrup had been stored there. There would be no Syrup Suckers and that would be the end of that. I asked Mr. Johnson and my parents if I could spend a night in the syrup container room. Mr. Johnson assured my parents that the Vermont Syrup Suckers had never hurt a person and, in fact, they were very shy.

So, a few nights later, there I am, all bundled up in my new winter parka, hiding in the corner of the container room watching the containers, pretty sure I won't see anything. The room is actually warm from the warm containers, and the air is sweet with the smell of maple syrup. Of course, I fell asleep. But then something wakes me. At first, I am afraid I might have missed it. And then I see something. It's two eyes. I never believed they existed but this one is staring right at me. I scream, I couldn't help myself, and the eyes disappear. I run out of the container room and into Mr. Johnson's house and wake up him and Mrs. Johnson screaming, "I saw it. It's out there!" Well, Mrs. Johnson seemed a little annoyed at being woken up but Mr. Johnson seemed a little amused. "Well I'm sure it is long gone by now. I know you didn't believe me, but now you know. Did you get a picture of it?" I admitted that I forgot my camera, and anyway as soon as I saw those eyes I just screamed and ran. After I calmed down a little Mr. Johnson got dressed and drove me back to our cheese house. I was determined to do a better job next time.

About a week later a new batch of warm syrup was being

prepared. This time I brought my camera and a flashlight. I was going to get a picture, if only of those eyes. I settled into my hiding place with a big bag of M&Ms that I was eating so that the sugar would keep me awake. Plus, I love M&Ms. But of course, after about an hour I fell asleep again. And again, something woke me, but this time I was ready. I slowly aimed my camera and pointed my flashlight right into those big eyes, and then, the Vermont Syrup Sucker started laughing. It was my rotten brother, dressed all in black, with a black hood over his head with two eye holes that had glittery paint all around them that made them look so gigantic.

I guess I was both angry and a little relieved to find out that Vermont isn't filled with invisible monsters. But it is filled with practical jokers,

QUIXOTIC JONES

I t was one of those old smoky bars that opens when the bartender can get there and closes when the last bar stool is vacant. He was usually in the booth in the back and he arrived just after the bartender, but left at 7:00pm sharp. When asked how he had come by his arguably odd name, Quixotic Jones would put down his ever-present cigarette, look the questioner in the eye, and reply, "I earned it buddy!" He would then slide his long skinny body to the far side of the seat and, with his deep gravelly voice, add, "Sit down buddy, I'll tell you all about it." Usually the invitation was ignored and the person walked away.

This was my first encounter with the old man and I sat down on the opposite side of the scarred table. I studied this man of perhaps sixty-five, dressed in a very old, well-worn three-piece suit, complete with a faded colorful tie. His face was lined and narrow and needed a shave. His dark eyes were deeply recessed beneath heavy grey brows and his breath was an unpleasant mixture of cigarettes and beer. He spoke first. "Tilting at windmills, buddy. That's how you become quixotic. I've been to every damn protest march this city has had. My mother marched when I was still unborn. Then she carried me, pushed me in baby strollers and led me by the hand. She pulled me out of school and drove us all over town. I've been in marches to end the Vietnam War, stop the bombing, free the Chicago Seven, stop the unfair treatment of people of color, raise the minimum wage, elect this one, impeach that one, defend the rights of poor people, and who knows what else. And you know the results of all that marching? I've been kicked out of school, fired from jobs, spent time in jail and have no real friends. And did it accomplish anything? Hell no!

"So, buddy, buy me a beer will ya. It's about all I have left."

That was my introduction to Henry Flyberg, known locally as Quixotic Jones. Of course, I bought him a beer and, as the afternoon advanced, a pack of non-filtered Camels and a couple more beers.

In spite of his claim to have been kicked out of school, Henry actually had earned a master's degree in political science from NYU. His best friend, now deceased, had christened him "Quixotic Jones" years ago after they had both been arrested for trying to block the Macy's Thanksgiving Day Parade. Henry had added a month of jail time to his original twenty-four-hour sentence by yelling at the judge that there was only so much helium in the world and wasting it on balloons was madness.

Henry's mother had been a wealthy Upper East Side widow with nothing else in her life — aside from a large penthouse apartment and a substantial bank account — but her son and a conviction that she could change the world. She and Henry attended marches in Connecticut, New York, and New Jersey. Sometimes they carried signs, but more often they just shuffled along with the crowd. His mother always wore an old cloth coat that she had found on the street and had had fumigated and dry-cleaned. They were never arrested in Manhattan.

Sometimes a police captain would appear and escort them out of the march. "Good afternoon, Mrs. Flyberg. Why don't you and the boy let me give you a ride home? This thing is about over and you know how confusing it can get at the end." That kind of intervention kept them out of the riot that followed the garment workers' march.

Henry's mother died at home, in the penthouse, watching a march to eliminate poverty on her large color TV.

"Well buddy, the day my mother died I realized that I was at one of the forks you find in the road. I could continue marching or give it up and start a life of my own. I decided to try something new. I got myself back into school and studied political science. I figured maybe they'd teach me how to make changes from the inside. Well buddy, what they taught me was that unless you're part of the right bunch of people you don't get to make changes. And, it seemed, some changes are just never gonna get made. Well that was discouraging!"

After NYU Henry decided to try a different approach. He earned a teaching certificate and set about trying to educate the children of the elite to see the world through his eyes. He proceeded to get fired from six exclusive, and expensive, private schools in Connecticut, New York, and New Jersey. Then he tried teaching in public schools in the wealthier districts with pretty much the same result.

"Buddy, it was almost funny. They'd bring me into the school board's disciplinary committee and ask me why I was trying to introduce socialism and even communism into my classes. Then I'd point out that I was just reading from Thomas Paine, Henry Thoreau, the Declaration of Independence, the Constitution of the United States, and that kind of founding documents. They'd reply that was not what the parents were saying and blah, blah, blah, you're fired.

"After a few years of that nonsense I retired from teaching. There was nothing else to do but to go back to marching. That was when I got the Quixotic Jones nickname. Well I'm done with all that too. I started giving my money away a few years ago. Let someone else have a go at those windmills. I'm living in a cheap hotel up the block now that my money's about gone. I wonder what's next, buddy."

The afternoon had turned into early evening and as 7:00pm approached, Henry stood up, took the nearly empty cigarette pack plus the full one I had just bought for him, thanked me for the beer, tipped his hat to the bartender, and proudly strode out the door. I have no idea what was significant about 7:00pm.

I never saw Quixotic Jones again. When I returned to the bar a few weeks later, the booth in the back was empty. The bartender told me he hadn't seen Quixotic Jones for over a week. And there I was at another one of the forks you find in the road. Should I start searching for Henry and be ready to deal with whatever I found, or just let him go? I've always felt a little guilty that I decided to just get on the train and return to Connecticut. I've never been much for tilting at windmills.

CANNIBALS

Sir Charles Peasely Skiffington rose majestically from the hand-carved dark oak chair at the head of the long linen covered table, slowly surveyed his twelve guests, elegantly raised his glass and proposed a toast. "To our dear ladies, may they continue to overlook our faults, but not forget us entirely." Which was followed by general polite laughter and then a shuffling of chairs as the six gentlemen also stood and lifted their glasses, each to his respective spouse.

"To our ladies!"

"And now, I believe my charming wife Eunice has prepared a special treat for all you lovely ladies, if you will just follow her into the drawing room. We, your devoted husbands, will smoke a cigar and after some boring discussions will join you later." With a rustle of finely fashioned fabric, six ladies rose from their chairs and followed Lady Skiffington out of the dining room and into the spacious, well-lit drawing room, eager to discover what entertaining amusement their hostess had provided.

As the doors to the drawing room closed, Sir Charles opened a polished mahogany cigar box, which Carter, the butler, had placed on the table. He then removed a dark brown specimen, held it up to his ear, and slowly rolled it between his thumb and first two fingers. "Still fresh gentlemen; please help yourselves, Carter has a sharp knife and will provide a light." The cigar box was then carried around the table. Cigars were selected, snipped, and set alight. The room became almost still except for the sounds of smoke being exhaled by seven well fed and now very relaxed gentlemen. Sir Charles pushed back his chair, looked at the burning tip of his cigar and spoke.

"Make yourselves comfortable gentlemen. I mean to tell you a most interesting story. It's about someone we all know, Nesbit Perkins. Just to refresh your memories, the Perkins family made their fortune two generations ago importing exotic spices and native art from the islands of the South Seas. Somehow Old Perkins, Nesbit's grandfather, got an exclusive contract from the royal family which put his company in control of a certain class of goods. If it came into England, Old Perkins got a cut, even if he had never laid hands or eyes on the stuff. Nice deal, what? But I was talking about Nesbit. What I'm sure you all must remember about him is the beautiful, very young wife he acquired on a trip to Sweden. I have never quite decided if she saw anything other than the Perkins fortune in poor Nesbit, but she was always the ideal wife, at least to all outward appearances. And why do I say poor Nesbit?"

"Indeed, Sir Charles! With a beautiful young thing like that about I'd be hard pressed to consider myself poor –and of course there was the Perkins fortune. And gentlemen, I beg you, do not repeat what I just said anywhere near my wife's hearing. That would not be good."

"Henry, you needn't worry on that account. I dare say each of us felt much the same on our first encounter with Mrs. Perkins. Those large bright blue eyes, that flawless alabaster skin, the softly draping golden blond hair, her amazing …but

I digress. Lucinda, for that is, in fact, Mrs. Perkins's Christian name, was a flirt. There, I've said it and I mean no disrespect to Nesbit or Lucinda herself. She was just too charming for her own or certainly Nesbit's good. She could walk into a room and somehow immediately abandon Nesbit, swept away as she was by both male and female admirers. I have always thought that the female admirers fell into two groups: those single women who were trying to figure out how Lucinda was able to so easily capture all the men, and the married women who were damned if they were going to let their husbands spend too much time with Lucinda."

"I plead guilty, and every minute was well worth the ride home with my charming wife's comments on the subject. Did Carter run off with the brandy or have you hidden it at your end of the table?"

"Would someone please send this bottle down to Sir David? A Welshman lacking drink is a sad thing indeed. Now, where was I? Oh yes, Lucinda's habitual flirting. I came to the realization that Nesbit didn't really mind his wife's intense socializing. His attitude seemed to be 'She's a beauty, isn't she? Well enjoy her, but just remember, chaps, she's coming home with me.' And of course she always did. I can honestly say that I have never heard even the slightest suggestion that Lucinda's flirting extended anywhere beyond the public gatherings."

"Oh, now, what about that story about young Freemont and Lucinda? Surely you heard that?"

"Please, please, please. Consider the source of that story. Young Freemont, indeed! The boy thinks he's some eighteenth century rake trying to drink and wench his way through daddy's fortune. I think we can safely ignore anything that comes out of that poor braggart's mouth. I'm sure that each of us wishes, in some dark place within us, that it was true, except not of course with young Freemont. But now, really, I haven't even gotten to the beginning of the story.

"You may know that Nesbit's favorite pastime was hunting grouse. And you may know he was a crack shot and owned several beautiful, and very accurate, shot guns. Those of you that also enjoy this activity may recall that two years ago, because of weather and whatever else makes grouse produce more little grouse, people were expecting the following grouse season to be exceptional. Well, unbeknownst to Nesbit, Lucinda had arranged a very elaborate surprise to celebrate Nesbit's fortieth birthday. They were to embark on a two-month cruise of the very same South Seas islands where Nesbit's grandfather had amassed the family fortune. After all that planning by his beloved wife, Nesbit really didn't have a choice. Some of you were fortunate enough to attend the Bon Voyage party that Lucinda had also created. All I can say is that it is a wonder that the ship sailed only an hour behind schedule. Everyone had to go on board and see the beautiful stateroom Lucinda had selected for their passage. It was actually two normal rooms with a sliding door between them. This was so that Nesbit could rise early to take the morning air while Lucinda slept soundly. Also, I expect, Lucinda just needed the extra space for all the clothes she had brought. There were two hundred first-class passengers and she intended to meet each one of them.

"Well, the ship set off at last and Lucinda was, of course, the belle of the ball. She left Nesbit to walk the decks and explore the ship's navigation centers while she set about mingling with the upper crust. She had even arranged a private tour for Nesbit of the entire below decks engineering spaces because she knew Nesbit fancied himself a bit of a technical man. She ate at a different table every meal and simply lost track of Nesbit.

"After the long journey, the ship returned at last to South-ampton and the passengers assembled, preparing to disembark. Lucinda appeared at the head of the gangway, surrounded as always by her many newfound friends. I was waiting on the dock to greet the returning couple and had, at Lucinda's insis-tence, arranged an elaborately decorated horse drawn carriage to take them to the bridal suite in the Royal Hotel. There they would remain for a few days to get used to being on land, and I hoped Lucinda planned to get reacquainted with her husband who, I suspected, she had pretty much ignored while at sea.

"As I watched, there appeared to be some confusion on the ship. Lucinda was anxiously crying to the captain 'Well, where is he? He must be someplace.' She then spotted me at the foot of the gangplank and pushed her way through the crowds, down the walkway, to literally throw herself into my arms."

"Here, here!"

"Will someone stifle that Welshman?"

"Well, as I looked down into those blazing blue eyes and watched her rapidly moving luscious pink lips, it took all my concentration to actually listen to what she was saying."'Sir Charles, something horrible has happened. I cannot find Nesbit. In fact I can't remember the last time I saw him. Could he have been eaten by the cannibals on one of those little islands? I had arranged trips for him to go visit the natives. Did they eat him?"'I tried to reassure her. 'Mrs. Perkins, please. I'm sure Nesbit has not been eaten by cannibals. I don't believe there even are any cannibals still in those islands. We both know your Nesbit; he'll turn up, don't you worry. Let's get you off to the hotel. Your two maids are waiting there for you. Then, I'll gather your trunks and see if I can find Nesbit.'

"I put her, alone, into the horse drawn carriage, having first convinced the captain and the first officer and the head of Barkley's bank that she would be fine with her personal carriage driver and two grooms outside and did not need further accompaniment on the short ride to the hotel. I then went looking for Nesbit. I interviewed the captain and the first officer, both of whom had much to say about the very charming Mrs. Perkins but weren't sure where they had last seen her husband. The captain called for the first-class steward but he had already gone ashore, as had most of his staff. I wandered about the now empty ship but could find no trace at all of Nesbit. I began to seriously wonder if he had, in fact, been eaten by cannibals."

Sir Charles relit his cigar, which had gone out as he was telling his tale, and refilled his brandy snifter from the decanter that had, fortunately, found its way back to his end of the table. He slowly looked around the room, a large grin spreading across his bearded face.

"Well, can you guess the outcome?'

"We are all in misery trying to figure it out. Please get on with it Sir Charles!"

"Well no one ever said Nesbit wasn't a clever man. He knew his wife very well and he knew how things would go on board that ship. He anticipated that she would enjoy every minute of it, and since he trusted her never to exceed the bounds of acceptable society, he slipped off the ship as the final caterers went ashore after the Bon Voyage party, and had a fine time grouse hunting in Wales. He had intended to meet the ship on its arrival, but couldn't tear himself away from one last day in the grouse infested Powys Hills. He did, at last, show up at the Royal Hotel two days after Lucinda's arrival. What happened then, I've not been told."

PINEAPPLES

Mr. Lee

Each day I must walk past the pineapple juggler. He is a foolish and sad man. I have tried to have him arrested or moved off that busy corner. I am told he has been there so long that the Chamber of Commerce granted him a special permit. They say the tourists expect him to be there and get upset if he is not. They are all foolish. The pineapple juggler's daughter, Karman, deserves better. She works for me at the Big Hawaiian Luau and I try to take care of her. I have plans.

The juggler worries me. He has now added a large machete to his act. First, he juggles just pineapples, sometimes five at once. It must hurt his hands. Then he drops two or three pineapples and adds his machete. You would think it must be dull. No. At the end he slices two of the pineapples in midair. He passes the pieces to the tourists. I tell the Chamber of Commerce this is dangerous. Someone will get hurt. They tell me "Go away, the tourists love him." They are all foolish people.

I know that sweet Karman deserves better, and that I am the only person in her world who can help her. The same way I helped her mother.

Karman

Like I know that working at the Big Hawaiian Luau isn't what I want to do forever. I mean, I know it's, like, just dumb. So, like, every day after high school, I'm off to the Luau. First, it's put on a really gross apron and start mixing Mai Tais. But, like, there's almost no rum and lots of sugar. Someone told me there's supposed to be something else. Not here. So, then the worst. Put on my hula costume. Can you believe? I'm the skinniest, whitest hula girl out there. The owner, Mr. Lee, says it makes me stand out. Ya think? Ten minutes of "The Authentic Island Welcome Dance," which is, like, shake your ass and move the grass. Oh, and smile for all the cell phones. You'd think that ought to be enough, right? No way. Then I'm a waitress for the "Original Hawaiian Feast": Pulled pork, poi, and pineapples. Like, the three 'Ps' of nutrition, right? By the time we've cleaned up and I get home, like, I barely have time to do some home-work and fall into bed. Mr. Lee pays us in cash at the end of the week. Like, I'm sure there's something wrong with that. But some weeks he gives me extra. So, cash is good, right?

But I have a plan. Every year Mr. Lee, who, like, is a creepy old dude, picks five or six girls for the mainland. Like he owns another one of these places in Los Angeles? I guess for people who don't want to come out to the islands. Maybe it's not, you know, exactly like Hawaiian Luau, but it's the same idea, I think. But, like, the best part is that after you're in Los Angeles for six months you're a resident. That means free college, or almost free. I'm not sure. So the plan is get picked for the mainland, work for six months and save everything. Then I quit, get my own apartment, and go to UCLA. I don't know what I want to major in. But, like, you don't have to make up your mind right away. I'm pretty sure.

So, like, Dad will miss me but he's getting really like odd? Some nights he walks around the house and talks to my mother? But, like, she's been gone for ten years? So he might not notice I'm gone. That'd be good.

Tyrone

Sometimes, now, I get confused. Those times when I'm having a conversation with Karman's mother I wonder if she's really there or if I am only imagining that she is there. And when I have that thought, exactly when I first have the start of that thought, she smiles at me, whispers, "Bye bye," and then she's gone. I wonder where she goes. She used to work at the Big Hawaiian Luau but then, without any discussion that I can recall, it seemed as if something changed and she wasn't around that much. And some of her stuff was gone, I think. And of course, we never sleep in the same bed anymore and I really miss that because that's how we got started, sleeping in the same bed. That's how Karman got started too. No, I don't mean that Karman and I used to sleep in the same bed. Or did we? When she was very little, when her mother stopped coming around, maybe then? How long ago was that? How old is Karman now? She's older than ten or eleven, I'm sure of that. She still goes to school, but it's a special school for special children, girls only I think, and it goes all day and into the night. She doesn't get home until it's bedtime, but then she has to do all the homework that she gets at the special school. I've tried to ask her what she's learning but she just jokes and says things like "Hula Dancing" and "Smiling for tips." I think that must be some of the young people's humor.

I don't understand it and her mother won't explain it to me on those few times I get to talk to her. I'm never sure when she will show up.

In my dreams there is an evil Chinese man named Mr. Lee who is trying to take away my pineapples so I can't juggle and will starve to death. That's why I added the machete to my act, so that if I ever see him on the street I can kill him before he gets my pineapples. Someone said there is a pineapple with a big diamond in it. When I finally find the diamond pineapple, I can stop working and retire. Maybe Karman will be finished with her special school and we can go visit the mainland. I haven't been back there for sixty years. Is it really that long? Maybe not. I'm not even that old. Sometimes I get confused.

Mr. Lee

These young girls are so stupid. They can count the number of tourists who pay fifty dollars each for watered down drinks, a pathetic meal, and a ridiculous show. They know how much I pay them, but they never sit down and figure out that I could triple their salaries and I'd still be making big money. But they're kids and their parents are mostly uneducated and working too hard themselves to pay much attention. And none of them has a clue about what happens when I send their daughters to the "mainland." They all believe the girls are going to Los Angeles. Well some of them are. Some go to Las Vegas, some to New York, some to New Orleans, wherever there is money looking for pretty girls. Most of the girls adjust quickly and those who don't, well they have to survive somehow. I think Karman will do very well. Her mother saved her money and now has her own flower shop in Las Vegas. It can be done.

Karman

Like, bummer? Just when I was, like, about to get off the island, my crazy father goes psycho and attacks Mr. Lee. And, like, kills him? And then, like double bummer, the cops find out that Mr. Lee has been sending girls to be prostitutes? Like yuck?! And so, they close the Big Hawaiian Luau and we are all out of a job. And my dad isn't going to jail because everyone says he was, like, just doing his act with the pineapples and the machete and Mr. Lee was, like, pushing his way through the crowd. So, someone pushes back on Mr. Lee, and like, he trips and gets right in the middle of Dad's pineapples just as Dad swings the machete to split the pineapple. Only Dad cuts Mr. Lee's head off. And now that I know what Mr. Lee was planning for me, I think he really got, like, what he deserved. But still, like yuck.

TWO RAVENS

wo black ravens on a faded red background marked the
pub's entrance. He could hear the sign over the entrance
swinging slowly back and forth long before he rounded
the corner. He thought to himself, *How many years have I walked
down this street, listening to the same creaking? First alone, then all
those wonderful years with Bridget, and now for two years alone again.*
Two unoiled hinges calling to him still. Some nights he found
himself matching his pace to the song of the ravens. Tonight was
a dark night, but the street lamps and the small light shining on
the ravens were sufficient to guide him to his destination.

As he reached to pull the door open it suddenly swung
towards him, opened wide, and presented Nancy O'Connell
framed in the soft light of the interior. "Hello Tim," she said as
she took a short step back to allow him to come in. "Tommy and I
were just leaving." They were both out the door and gone before
Tim could manage even a simple "Evening." *I wonder where they're
off to in such a rush* he thought *but I suppose I know.* And again, he
realized how he missed his Bridget. Stumbling a bit, he crossed
from the dark entrance towards the bar.

It was only when he reached the long empty bar that Tim
realized that there were no other drinkers standing there. The time

was at least an hour before last call, but aside from himself and Michael the barkeep, the room appeared to be empty. He turned slowly around, peering into the darker corners where couples often sat to be by themselves, but found no one anywhere. And the room was deathly quiet.

"Michael," he asked, "where the devil is everyone? Is my watch broken? Is it already after closing?"

Michael, who was half Tim's age but twice as large, leaned across the bar and spoke in a surprisingly soft voice. "I'm thinkin' it might just be that new Sports Bar a block over. They have big tellys hangin' on every wall and they're showing some big football match. People are over there payin' twice what I charge 'em for drinks and havin' a royal good time. Or, maybe something else is going on."

Neither spoke for a minute and the ravens swung outside. "So Tim, do ya think I ought to oil those hinges? Mrs. Dolan across the way says the noise keeps her awake all night, which is a bit daft because we all know she's deaf as a post."

Tim smiled. "Michael, if those birds ever stopped singin' to me I'd never be able to find the place. Now, would you please pour me a pint and tell me the latest gossip?" Michael walked off to fill a beer glass and Tim was again strongly aware of being alone. Michael returned carrying a full beer glass and a small whiskey glass.

"Here ya go, and I brought you a little Jameson to warm you up. And I'm buyin' tonight, just for you. Now as to the gossip, hmmm. You heard about Brendan and…"

"Oh God yes! I heard. It was disgusting. And I already know what they're saying about Sister Dymphna over at the convent. That poor old woman."

There was a pause as Tim addressed the whiskey and again

46

surveyed the darkened empty room. He spoke. "Ya know, it is positively strange being in here when it's so quiet. Should we be listenin' for ghosts? You're a bit new here, but the last fella was older than I am and he swore the place was haunted."

"Tim, you know I been here almost twenty-five years now."

"What I said, you're kinda new. You know who knew ghosts? My dear wife Bridget, god I miss her. She'd be the one to have here tonight. She used to talk about her Ma and her granny, said Granny used to talk to her ma for years after Granny passed. And then after her ma died Bridget sometimes would get an odd look on her face and laugh. I'd ask her what she was laughing at and she'd just say 'Oh, it's just Ma,' and then she'd give me her mysterious face and I'd just have to cross the room and kiss her. Well, I guess all the ghosts are gone with her. Maybe if we'd had a daughter, she could have carried it on."

There was another quiet pause then Tim looked back at Michael. "Could I get a little more of that Jameson? I'll even pay for it."

An even thicker silence seemed to fill the room as Michael moved down the bar. Tim could not remember ever before being in this place alone with only a barkeep for company. It was the complete lack of noise that was so different. But then he realized that he had, after all, been here many times and been unaware of a single sound. He and Bridget would sit together in one of the dark corners, holding hands and staring into each other's eyes, hearing nothing at all of the outside world. Even after they had been married for years, there were nights when Michael, having closed the bar, wiped down the tables and sent the other stragglers home, then had to break into Tim and Bridget's silence and herd them out the door. Tim missed those nights.

Tim raised the Jameson and held it in front of him. "Michael, do you remember those rare times when Bridget and I might have had a bit more than usual? I'd say to her 'My dear I believe you are soused.' And she'd come right back with, 'So are you, you damn fool.'"

Michael laughed "Ha! Oh yes, those very rare occasions. And then you two would start hugging and kissing like teenagers. I sometimes was almost ready to dump a bucket of cold water on you. And you bein' the age of my parents! Oh, I do remember. 'And so are you, you damn fool.' I can hear her sayin' it."

Tim turned away from the bar, perhaps staring at one of the dark corners. "Oh we weren't that bad were we?" Hearing no reply he turned back and Michael was not there. Had he gone off to start closing up the pub? The lights over the bar seemed dimmer and the outside light over the ravens was now darkened. He could still hear the sign creaking in the evening's soft breeze. He sat there in the deepening darkness, thinking he should be leaving, when he noticed a motion in one of the corners. Someone was over there. The person was too small to be Michael.

"Hello Tim." He knew the voice but also knew it could not be her. He dearly wished it could, but no. And then it was. Bridget emerged from the dark and crossed the room to stand in front of him. Her hair hanging long and black as it was when she was a girl. Her eyes still an intense blue that penetrated his soul. Any hesitation or fear he might have felt was overcome by a rush of joy, happiness, and love. Somehow, by some magic, Bridget was there. He dared not try to touch her for fear of breaking the spell. He tried to speak but only managed "But Bridget, my love... you're dead."

She smiled, came closer, extended her arms and softly spoke. "And so are you...you damn fool."

CLIFDEN

The man behind the bar was large, well over six feet tall, with wide shoulders. A wreath of curly red hair and a bright red beard gave him the appearance of some ancient sun god. His warm greeting, however, immediately melted away our initial hesitation upon entering the pub. No matter who he actually was or where we were, it appeared we had a friend.

"Well, you three better come in and sit down. Try that table over there, by the window. Nice view of the castle from there. And I'm thinkin' you'll be wantin' a bit of something to settle you down. I'm guessin' Guinness for the gentleman, some white wine for the lady, and tea with lemon and honey for the little miss?"

Coming from a man we had never met, in a pub we had never entered or even seen before, it seemed just the next strange event in an ongoing series. He was, of course, correct on every point; we were in a mild state of shock and those were exactly the drinks we would have ordered. I nodded a firm yes in his direction and the three of us moved towards the table by the window, from which we could just see the taller towers of Clifden Castle.

The morning had started very early. It never gets completely dark in Ireland in early July. All three of us were wide awake when the clock still said 4:00 AM. My wife and daughter and I were in our second day in the rented house in western Ireland. The first day had been spent driving from the airport, sleeping and then walking along the narrow winding road in front of our house. The road was bordered on both sides with old stone walls, and the fields beyond the walls contained the walls of even older stone houses which had long ceased to provide shelter for the local farmers and their families. An occasional small herd of dairy cows would sometimes wander over to see if we had brought anything special for them. In the distance, across the softly rolling green fields we could see flocks of sheep, each one marked with a splash of bright spray paint to identify their owner. Today's goal was a drive through the Connemara Mountains, a visit to Kylemore Abbey, and a stop in Clifden. There was mention of something called Clifden Castle and all of us, my young daughter especially, were curious as to what that could be.

My daughter, who had just turned thirteen, was still an imaginative child. She could spend the entire morning happily building elaborate "Fairy Houses" in the woods, hoping they might be inhabited during the night. Ireland was, for her, a place of magic and leprechauns. She was also convinced that the pubs in Ireland were the same as bars at home and that she would get in big trouble if she dared to enter one, even with her parents.

After a breakfast of oatmeal, Irish soda bread, and tea we set out. Once upon a time I was a relaxed person who didn't really worry about much. That must have been before I finished graduate school, got a job, and found myself with a wife and child.

When you realize that you are not the only one for whom you are responsible, your attitude changes. At least mine did. For our trip to Ireland I was worried about the rental car and driving in strange places and ever finding the tiny village of Cashel way out past Galway. Did we have enough money? Would the ATM machines accept our cards? Would thieves steal our passports? What are you supposed to do if you run over someone's sheep? Oh, and is everyone having a good time?

In Ireland they drive on the "wrong" side of the road and the cars have the steering wheel on the right side. You shift with your left hand, but the pedals are at least in the normal place. As long as the road is straight without too many oncoming cars it isn't too difficult, until you come to a rotary, or as they call them, "roundabouts." Think about it; you are going clockwise on the left side of the road. Adding to the driving excitement are the narrow winding roads, often closely bordered by high, thick hedges, and the fact that Irish van drivers come down the middle of the road going as fast as possible. And then every now and then you come around a corner and confront a flock of color-coded sheep or perhaps a couple of cows or maybe an entire herd of cows, all moving very slowly across or sometimes even along the road. Twenty minutes of this makes the driver very happy to pull into whatever tourist stop has a parking lot. We made many stops, drank a lot of tea, and ate many buttery scones that morning. It doesn't sound bad when you put it that way.

Fortunately, my wife was the sensible one. She didn't get stressed when driving, even on the wrong side of the road. She was also able to calm me down when I was getting upset about driving or traffic or just getting lost. She had even been able to convince our daughter that, since they served lots of food in pubs, children were invited and would not be arrested.

Kylesmore Abbey is now a very posh school for young ladies, but there are sections open for tourists and I think the school was out of session for the summer. Next to the abbey is a small cathedral built for a family with much too much money as their own private place to worship. There was also a beautiful view back across a lake to the Connemara Mountains and, of course, more tea and scones. It was late in the afternoon when we finally arrived at Clifden. We walked around town and visited the shops, bought a nice sweater and all agreed to avoid anything that looked as if it might serve tea and scones. Finally, we found Visitor Information and asked about Clifden Castle. A very young-looking woman seemed to hesitate slightly before turning to look at the clock on the wall in back of her and then saying, "Well I guess you've got time before the fog." She then proceeded to give us directions to Castle Road, which was just off the main road but, she noted, probably wouldn't be marked because the local teenagers seemed to think "Castle" made an excellent trophy to hang on their bedroom door.

We followed her directions (she was correct, there was no sign) and turned down what we hoped was, in fact, Castle Road. The road itself appeared to have been recently resurfaced and was in excellent shape, except for being very steep and narrow and lined with tall trees and hedges. Fortunately, we didn't encounter anyone coming up and we soon found ourselves at a small parking lot adjacent to a section of beach. There was one other car, but no sign of any people and no sign of any castle. There was a path leading through the tall grass, heading down the beach so, with no alternative, we followed it.

Very soon we came to a large wooden and wire fence which ran right across our path and into the water. However, there were steps going up one side and down the other. It took me a moment, but then I realized that the fence was to control livestock, not people. I think the stairs are called stiles. There was a small brass plaque attached to the top step containing the words "Hyacinth's Gate." We descended the other side and moved up another stretch of beach. The next steps over a fence were labeled "Joyce the Butcher," and the steps after that were labeled "Thomas Eyre's Gate." The next one had a tag labeled "Charles Eyre's Gate." What turned out to be the last one was labeled simply "D'Arcy." A few yards past that fence we could see the castle off to our right across a wide green pasture. There were several paths leading up to it and we followed the first one we came to. We could see a couple of cows in the distance, but they didn't seem at all interested in us so we hurried up to the castle, being careful to avoid stepping in any of the cow plops along the way.

The castle's grey stonework appeared to be in excellent repair, but there was no sign of the roof or any roof beams. There were openings for windows but again, no sign of window frames or even any sign of broken frames or any wooden or metal frame pieces at all. A large front wall rose at least four stories and was completely covered with bright green ivy. There were several towers, but no stairs existed that allowed exploring anything other than the ground level. We wandered through the various rooms and were aware of the complete lack of any tourist related plaques, or any sort of visitor accommodations at all. There certainly was no offer of tea and scones. My daughter enjoyed peering into the many window openings, hoping to find something magical in each room. We found one large section which appeared to have been set up as some sort of cow or sheep pen. It still contained piles of manure from both animals and we didn't get too close. Finally my daughter found the one brass plaque that existed. It was on the wall next to what looked to have once been either a small fireplace, or more probably an oven.

It turned out that Clifden Castle was built not by a king, but by the man who essentially built and owned Clifden and most of the land around it. John D'Arcy had his castle built in 1818 and he lived in it until his death in 1839, six years before the Irish potato famine started. During his life he was supported by the tenants of his land from whom he collected rents, and one assumes food and whatever labor he required. After his death the castle and estate were ruled by his son, Hyacinth, who was unable to successfully manage the tenants even before the famine hit. The entire estate, again including all of what is now the town of Clifden, went into decline, but then was purchased by two brothers from England, Thomas and Charles Eyre, in 1850. In the midst of Irish starvation, they felt they needed a "holiday retreat" from whatever was making them rich in Bath. The castle remained inhabited, at least for part of the year, until 1894 when it was abandoned. It was later bought in 1917 by J.B. Joyce, a local butcher, much to the outrage of the local tenants who had continued using the land and treating it as their own. After a lengthy court battle, which resulted in the butcher getting some of his purchase price back, ownership was given over to the tenants' association. Immediately the tenants removed all the roofing, roof timbers, internal timbers, window glass, and frames, and sold the lot of it. The castle has remained in a state of ruin surrounded by pastureland ever since.

By now the fog was rolling up from the sea and over the pasture and we hurried back down the path towards the beach. We could barely see ten feet in front of us as we headed back to the car, passing up and over each stile very carefully. Finally we came to a long stretch of beach. The parking area looked different in the fog, and then we realized that we did not see our car. We did not see the other car that had been there either. Staying close to each other, and with a feeling of anxiety, we continued searching until my daughter called out "Is this the road back?" She had come across what looked to be the road we had come down, but now the bottom section seemed to be covered with sand. Had the tide come up and gone out while we were at the castle? That didn't seem right, but this certainly seemed to resemble the road, except for it being sand covered and not newly paved. I was getting very upset at this point. Had the people in that other car waited for us to leave and then stolen our car? What were we supposed to do now? There must be police in Clifden, Guardia they are called. How would we get back to our rental house? My daughter and wife both tried to calm me down. My daughter was hoping we had gone through some magic doorway at the castle or in the fog and were going to have a great adventure. My wife was, I thought, more sensible. "Hey, we're lost. Maybe someone stole the car, but it can't have been the first time. I'm betting there is a standard form, 'Tourist Car Stolen at Beach,' waiting at the police station. All we have to do is find the police station."

So, with no other obvious options, we started up the sand covered road. I was hoping to find that nice new blacktop around every turn. Well, once the sand stopped, the road was just dirt and I started wondering if perhaps my daughter was right after all. I was completely out of breath and on the edge of panic when we reached the main road at the top and read the sign on the road we had just come up: "Butcher." In my condition that sounded ominous, but across the main road we could see a pub and we hurried into it. It was at this point that the barman correctly guessed our choice of drinks and pointed out the table near the window. The pub was well lighted and presented a sharp contrast to the foggy dimness outside. We sat.

The waitress was small, not much taller than my daughter. A woman in her thirties, she wore a black turtleneck sweater over black slacks and looked as if she should be a stagehand. She had one long, thick black braid draped over her left shoulder. Her blue eyes sparkled as she set down the drinks tray and introduced herself. "Hello, I'm Kate, and you looked confused."

As she set out our drinks, she took a long look at me and said, "And you've just come up Butcher's Way and think you might be in the Twilight Zone, am I right? No, don't answer. Enjoy your drinks and all will be revealed." And she spun around and departed. I'm not that big a beer drinker but I really think it is possible that I swallowed the entire pint in one gulp. Even my wife was amazed.

Kate returned with a second pint, which she placed before me, pulled up and straddled an empty chair, and began. "The wits at the Tourist Info sent you down to the castle as the fog was comin' in, didn't they? And then they forgot to tell you to count the stiles on the way back. I don't know why they pay those people. Missy, do you know what stiles are?"

My daughter proudly answered, "Yes. They are those steps that go over the fences."

"Right! And did you see the brass tags with the names on them?"

"Yes, and then we saw the big plaque at the castle. Those tag names were all the people who once owned the castle."

"That's very good, young lady. And what was the name of the first stile you crossed?"

"Hyacinth, he was Mr. D'Arcy's son."

"And when you came back, did you read the labels again?"

"No, we were hurrying and there was all that fog."

And then Kate gave me a long penetrating look before speaking. "Okay Dad, now here's your question. What did you do wrong and how did you get here?"

And of course, it finally hit me. I felt foolish, but so relieved I almost dropped the pint. "We only made it back to the Butcher and stumbled onto Butcher's Way, which is the dirt road we came up to get here."

"And now for the grand prize, sir, what must be the name of this pub?"

"Well what else could it be than 'The Butcher's?'" "Correct, sir. And for that you and your family win a free ride back to your car, which is parked right where you left it. My brother Sean is keeping an eye on it and if you were to drop five pounds on him for his efforts, I'm sure he wouldn't mind."

I finished the pint, paid for our drinks, with a nice tip for Kate, and she gave us all a ride back to our car. I was happy to give Sean ten pounds, and, in fact, he didn't seem to mind. I let my wife drive us back to the Clifden Hotel, where we consumed a fine dinner before returning, uneventfully, to our rented house in Cashel.

MOON MUSHROOMS

Just as I got back from the moon it was time for dinner. Seems as if that always happens. Still sipping daintily from her second bourbon martini, Mom bounced off the walls in the hallway, made her way into the kitchen, stared blurry-eyed at the week's menu, pushed a few buttons, and dinner appeared on the table. Pop, who only drank beer, threw his brand new copy of the *Saturday Evening Post* on the floor and muttered almost incoherently "Why don't they just let Norman Rockwell write the whole thing?" Doesn't he always say that? Then sis slid down her pole from Up Above right into her adult sized highchair. Was her skin always that dark? Home sweet home at last.

I don't really like any of these people, but I have always believed that they were my family. So, I endure. What else?

Picking mushrooms on the moon is a strange job that didn't even exist when I was a little tyke, or so they tell me. I'm still not sure how it works, but I guess it pays the bills. Pop hasn't worked since he was laid off from his job as a dog walker at McDonalds. It seems as if Mom and sis couldn't stay focused long enough to perform even an hour's real work. I think Mom interviewed for a job as Fat Lady at the circus when she was pregnant with me but she wasn't fat enough. Sis tried out for a cheerleader job but wasn't nearly cheerful enough.

Oh look, that guy. He's supposed to be my brother, and is supposedly just back from picking mushrooms on the moon. That can't really be a job. And he looks different from the last time he was here. Well good. Now he can be the center of attraction for those two deranged old people and I can resume my search for alien life in green vegetables. I'm positive there really are little green men and I don't understand why anybody would think they live on Mars. Isn't Mars the "Red Planet?" Duh! I think it's kale but I'll need a better magnifying glass to find them. Unless I decide to try hypnosis right on the little, little, little green men while they are still in the kale. Or maybe I'll just work on my tan or paint my toenails. Or maybe, I'll just do Appys or Zappys. "Appy to Zappy to keep you happy!"

It's that boy again. I think it's the same one, but there is always something a little different about him. Maybe I should start putting less bourbon in my martinis, or maybe more. How else am I supposed to get through the afternoon? Coffee in the morning, booze at night. Wait, what about the rest of the day. What do I do then? Oh, sit and watch and listen to something: Brad and Marsha, Tiffany and Melonie and Stan, all those people. And who are they? And why do I care? That boy, he always has that uniform. Is he a curator? That girl, every time she comes down the pole she has changed. Who is she? She seems to know the boy, maybe. And who the hell is the old man? At least he never changes. I'm so confused. But I'm always confused. Maybe that's what I'm supposed to be or do.

Mining mushrooms on the moon, ha! He really believes that, whichever one he is. Mushrooms on the moon, regular commuter traffic back and forth –what nonsense. I wonder where he has been and what he has really been doing. And now he thinks he is home to his family. How many different families are there? Do they all have an alcoholic middle-aged woman, a nubile idiot girl who changes every time she comes down the pole? Do they all have an old fart like me? God, maybe outer space aliens took over and we are all in a zoo. That Norman Rockwell sure could draw.

THE FULLER BRUSH MAN

G etting from one place to another has always been a problem for people. A long time ago a kid named Hojanias of the Botai people in Kazakhstan was the first person who, tired of walking, tried to ride one of the wild horses that lived in the area. He also did it to impress a girl. Of course, the horse threw him off; he broke his neck and died. The girl was not impressed. The rest of the village, however, realized that Hojanias might be on to something. They decided that the women should try to tame some of the horses. Not only did they tame them for riding, they also learned to milk the mares for a major addition to the tribe's diet. And soon the horse became the major method of transportation everywhere.

Science moved on and a guy named Galileo found himself wondering about the Earth and the sun and the moon and why a big rock and a little rock, when dropped from a tall tower, both hit the ground at the same time. Why didn't the heavier one get there first? And he figured out that the Earth actually circled the sun. That landed him in hot water. In 1642 Galileo died and the same year Isaac Newton was born. And people think these things happen by themselves. Isaac started wondering about the same things Galileo had been contemplating. Okay, the planets circled the sun in what were ellipses, not circles. But why did they do that? And why did the two rocks hit the ground at the same time? And he came up with an answer. "Let's say there is some magical force that pulls things together depending on how big they are and how far apart they are. Yeah, that's ridiculous—force at a distance—but it answers all our questions." And it did. Soon after that people, still riding on horses or in carriages pulled by horses wanted some way to go much further much faster. Some guys had built a gigantic machine that used the power of expanding steam to turn wheels and run factories. "Guys, maybe you could make a little one to turn the wheels of my carriage?"

And someone made a small steam engine and the Stanley Steamer went roaring down the road, scaring the dickens out of anyone within a mile. But we could now travel much further much faster, until the car ran out of water or fuel for the fire or the boiler just blew up. The gasoline engine soon followed, and Henry Ford put the world on the road. Back in the science labs people were still worrying about Newton's magical force-at-a-distance. It made no sense, but it was totally useful. "Force equals Mass times Acceleration," or a more useful way of looking at it, acceleration equals force divided by mass. In other words, the faster you want to go the harder you had to push and the lighter you wanted to be. And then Einstein came along and answered Newton's magic force-at-a-distance with an even more ridiculous suggestion. What we think of as "mass" warps the space-time-continuum and makes it appear that things are responding to a magic force. Right, and if you believe that I can get you a great deal on a bridge in Brooklyn. And just as the scientists were getting their heads wrapped around Relativity Theory—that's what Einstein called it—along come Quantum

Theory, Quarks, String Theory, Spaghetti Theory, and the search for the Higgs Boson, which is supposed to be at the base of what we used to call mass. Meanwhile, the average person in the street was driving a hybrid car and flying around in jet planes and watching rocket ships go to Mars. And that was the problem. While the astronomers were showing the world pictures of distant galaxies which might contain who knew what in the way of planets or life forms, the physicists were saying "Forget it! Those things are thousands of light years away and there is no way we can ever get there." It turns out that one of the nasty little results of Relativity Theory was that, yes, Newton's little formula for accelerating a certain amount of mass was pretty good as long as you weren't going very fast. But, it turns out that as you approach the speed of light, your mass starts to increase. What?! Yeah, so that means you can't get up to the speed of light without making your mass infinite and even Newton could tell you, when that happens you ain't goin' nowhere.

And there it stood. The Europeans built the CERN particle accelerator to go looking for the Higgs Boson and whatever else they could discover to make them even more confused. Stephen Hawking was wondering about black holes and then one day Max Friedstein, a leading CERN researcher who had been awake all night trying to make sense of the latest pile of data, ordered a cheese and onion omelet in the CERN cafeteria. As he was walking to a table, he tipped his tray. The plate slid to the edge and the omelet hit the flour, splitting open and sending bits of onion flying in all directions. Max watched it happen, dropped the tray, and screamed "Oh mein Gott! That's it!" And Inverse Black Hole Theory was born. It took them less than a year before the first probe went to the Andromeda Galaxy and returned. Round trip, two hours and thirteen minutes.

So here am I, a sort of galactic Fuller Brush Man. I go from inhabited planet to inhabited planet trying to bring each civilization what it needs. Some places I teach a couple of people how to make fire, some places I introduce the idea of zero as a placeholder. Whatever they need. I can't stop anything, although that would be nice. I think it was K52 in orbit around star ST0023MW where the entire population decided that they wanted to go to LaLa Land—a sort of afterlife heaven—that they all, every single one of them, killed themselves. If you'd be willing to clean up a whole lot of dead bodies, it's a pretty nice planet.

Of course, I stay in the Milky Way Galaxy. Those younger kids go out to Andromeda and even beyond. The stories they bring back would bend your head a little. One guy claims to have found the favorite planet of science fiction writers. The planet of beautiful women who are just waiting for a man to teach them about—well you get the idea. Kids! I don't know, I suppose anything is possible out there. And all this because Max couldn't keep his tray level.

Well, it's been nice chatting with you. No, I've got this.

WOODS

"These woods are lovely, dark and deep," said the poet, but he forgot to add, "and sometimes damn odd."

I was walking a trail that I had been enjoying for perhaps thrity-five years. When I had first encountered it, the path had been barely visible and it was necessary to carefully follow the blue blazes which were yearly updated by a local Boy Scout troop. But now after many new hikers had followed this route, the path was crossed by exposed roots and rocks. Even the thick fall covering of white and black oak leaves had by this spring day been ground into a soft brown dust. In many places, bare ground and even a small rain puddle might greet the walker. No longer did a hiker have to watch for the blazes. The worn trail was easy to follow. Of course this had not deterred the Boy Scouts from their sometimes overly enthusiastic blaze renewals.

I was walking alone and stopping occasionally just to enjoy the silence, broken only by the call of a single bird. On this June day the sun was already high in the sky and the canopy of oaks filtered its rays, allowing only rare patches of bright sunlight to reach the ground. I had completed the section furthest away from the road, and as a result the quietest, when I encountered another walker holding her young dog on a leash. I am slightly angered by the statewide requirement to leash dogs when you are walking them in the woods. I don't get it. There is some concern that someone's pet will attack another hiker. There is also a concern that the dog will somehow harm the wild animals that live in the woods. For all the years we owned our dog I let her run through these woods. She would sometimes smell a deer and take off for a romp. It was fun for both animals I'm sure. The deer knew she could kick the dog senseless if it ever got even close, and so did the dog. As for dogs attacking other walkers or their dogs, I am equally unconvinced. Our dog would often, on encountering another dog, go through the standard dog greeting which is along the lines of, "Hey, don't try anything. These are my people." Or on rarer occasions, our dog being spayed, "So, you want to fool around?" I never was attacked or even threatened by another dog and my dog never threatened or attacked anyone. I said "Hello" to the girl and, feeling sorry for her dog, moved on.

I continued along the path, and as I reached the section that runs along the road the stillness was broken by the sounds of a car, a pickup truck, and an airplane all converging into my auditory space at once. And then they were gone. I then started through a section of tall green ferns and that is where it happened. For some reason I looked down and to my right and there he was. He was a miniature man. My first thought was, *My god, I've had a stroke and I'm seeing things.* Before I could even react, he spoke, not in a little elfin voice, but sounding the same as a normal sized man. "Oops. Sorry, you weren't supposed to see me. I guess I didn't hear you after that noise with the airplane and all. Okay, before you ask, I'm a leprechaun but I don't have a pot of gold, and how are you today?"

I sat down on a nearby tree trunk and tried to make sense of the little creature I was looking at. A stroke still seemed to be the best explanation. I was just staring at him, completely at a loss for words. What do you say to a two-foot-tall leprechaun dressed not in green but in a Yankees T-shirt, LL Beans hiking shorts, and miniature Tevas boots? He had nothing on his head but black hair, which had been given a buzz cut.

"Aren't you going to speak? Has my appearance struck you dumb? I tried to dress in a locally acceptable costume. God, what I wouldn't give for a Guinness right now. I know; I saw the damn sign, NO ALCOHOLIC BEVERAGES. What is it with you people and alcohol?"

That last got me to thinking and I managed to respond. "So, what would you give for a Guinness right now?" As I had hoped it got his attention.

"I know you don't have one with you but what have you got in mind? I already told you I don't have a pot of gold. What idiot started that idea? Do you have any idea how heavy those things are? Wait, I didn't say that and you didn't hear it. So where were we? Oh yeah, wishes. Oh, if I could get rid of 'HIM' I would have long ago, so don't ask. And be careful. People are always wishing for things that get them in trouble. Just what kind of Guinness do you have, not that Blonde mouthwash or that goofy canned draught with the nitrogen golf balls in it?"

The guy clearly liked to talk. I guess he didn't get much chance. I assured him. "Six bottles of Guinness Extra Stout are there just waiting for you. And I have an idea for our bargain. I'm not asking for a wish. How about you make it so that none of my children or their children are significantly affected by climate change. My wife and I will probably be dead before it gets too bad, but they will have to live through some hard times."

"Deal!" He almost screamed. "Have you looked at your children lately? All of them are already so adaptable, intelligent and even well-traveled. And your grandchildren are being taught to take care of themselves without much outside help. This is too easy! So, where do you keep your Guinness?"

I had to ask. "How do you know so much about my family?" He looked up almost incredulously. "I'm a friggin leprechaun! I know stuff. Let's get a move on."

I decided to just head home and see if he would follow or I would wake up in the hospital being told a hiker had found me passed out on the trail. I didn't know if he planned to walk along with me or how he planned to cover the half mile to my house. I looked down and he was gone, but when I got home there he was, hiding behind a rock outside my back door. I went inside and brought out a bottle of Guinness Extra Stout and handed it to him. He looked at me as if I was an idiot. "Could you just remove the cap?" I did; he emptied it in one long gulp, gave me the empty and said, "Just one more for now, please." He dispatched the second bottle and then just disappeared. I rinsed out the two empties, threw them into the recycling, and ran to start typing this.

STRAWBERRIES

A few weeks ago, I noticed that my beard, which had been almost white, has rather suddenly returned to the rich red rust color it had when I was twenty-five. I reasoned that this not at all unpleasant surprise must have a cause, but what could it be? My list of medications had not changed, I had not changed my diet significantly and, given my history of precancerous basal cells on my skin, I was still avoiding direct sunshine as much as I could. It was not until I was trimming the lawn, pulling out dandelions and other weeds, that I realized that all spring I had been eating the small red wild strawberries which had started appearing in the lawn a few years ago. As strawberries go, they are not at all sweet and, to be honest, don't even have much taste. But they are pretty and just the name "wild strawberries" invokes images of Ingmar Bergman and his odd movies. How could I not pop the occasional little red berry into my mouth? Could they be the cause of my beard's revival? What could I do but consult Dr. Google?

As always, the internet was amusing. I found several names for the little berries and became unsure which names applied to the ones I was ingesting. Some sources suggested that with enough sugar they could be tasty. Of course, that's also true of crab grass. My favorite entry was from a now defunct "healthy foraging" journal which suggested that at least one version of these berries contained an as yet unidentified C vitamin which rejuvenates the body. I decided to go with that concept, continued eating the berries as I found them, and waited for at least a moderate Viagra effect. That never happened, for which my wife is certainly grateful.

I was trimming along the back woods line when, reaching down to pick a red berry, I saw a small hand reach out and grab it first. So, I grabbed the hand. I gently lifted a small creature out of the ferns and, still holding its wrist, set it on the grass at my feet. Before I could even say, "So, who or what are you?" a very female voice spoke to me.

"So, you're the Big. He said you had a beard, but he said it was white. But you've been stealing the berries. Naughty, naughty."

She was either an elf or another leprechaun, and since she seemed to know the leprechaun I had already met, I decide she was one. Her long shiny black hair was gathered in a ponytail and topped by a soft green beret. Her T-shirt had something written in Gaelic; she had Kelly green bib overalls and shiny black boots. If she had been five-feet-six instead of two-and-a-half-feet tall, she would have been quite sexy. I admit that it was the Lauren Bacall voice that really got to me. I asked "So, you must know the guy I met in the woods a few months ago. How many of you are living around here?"

She laughed. "Ha! None of us and all of us. You poor Bigs only live in one place at a time. How boring. But we have other things to talk about. First, would you stop eating our berries? You think they are strawberries. Well they're not. I notice your beard has gone back to its youthful glory. And I can only imagine what else you are anticipating. Trust me, you don't want what those berries are going to give you. But what we really have to discuss is how much Guinness did you give my son?"

"That was your son? You don't—" She stopped me there. "Don't start flirting with me boyo. Yes, he's my son and just how much stout did you give the poor lad? When he got home, he passed out and slept for a day. You must have let him have at least half a bottle."

What could I say? "Well, it might have been more than that."

"The boy's not yet fifty. You didn't let him have an entire bottle, did you?"I felt the need to look away, although I was still holding her tiny wrist. "Okay, I'll tell you the truth. We made a deal and he wanted a second bottle, so I gave it to him."

"What? You made a deal with an underage leprechaun? Did your mother never teach you anything? What kind of deal did you make? I'll see if I can get you out of it."

"Well, we were talking about nothing in particular when he happened to say 'What I wouldn't give for a Guinness.' So I asked him what he would do for one. But you should be proud of him; he warned me that most people who make deals with leprechauns live to regret it."

She sighed heavily for so tiny a person, and asked "So, what did you ask for?"

"I just asked him to take care of my kids and grandkids when climate change gets really bad. Um, and I told him I had at least six bottles of stout at home."

Somehow, I had let go of her wrist and she walked a few paces away, turned, looked up at me and with a wry smile asked, "And how did my wee son react to your request?"

"Well, he seemed quite pleased. He said that would not be

a problem because my children already knew how to take care of themselves and my grandchildren were being taught."

"And you believed he knew all about your family?"

"I did ask him about that, and he told me that because he was a leprechaun, he knew stuff. So, then he followed me home and I gave him two bottles of stout, at which point he disappeared."

"Well, mister, I'd say you got off lucky. In the first place, most leprechauns don't know anything about you Bigs or your families and my son doesn't know much about anything. So, when he comes back for the rest of the beer, please just tell him you talked to his mum and he better just forget about any more free Guinness." And with that, she was gone. How do they do that?

I have now stopped eating the wild strawberries and, as you can see, my beard is again white. And my wife is relieved about that other thing.

LULU

Lulu picked up the bar tab that had been placed in front of her, studied it a while, and then turned to the girl on her left. "Hey, I ain't payin' this. What the hell's a Rambo Shooter? Who ordered that? And what happened to the guys that brought us here? Trixie, what the f—?"

"Lulu! Stop talkin' like a hooker."

"Oh, and how do you know how hookers talk? Dooon't look at me like that. That was not what you thought it was. But, like I said, where are those guys and who's payin' this tab, 'cause it ain't me. Hey, bar guy! What happened to those guys we came in with?"

"I don't think you'll be seeing them again. Mr. Marcheti kinda escorted them out."

Lulu straightened a strap on her dress and replied, "Who the hell is Mr. Marcheti?" Almost immediately a voice from behind her spoke.

"I'm Mr. Marcheti, and you are?"

Lulu turned on the barstool and saw a well-dressed man wearing a black three-piece suit, a pink shirt, and a fancy painted tie. He looked to be her father's age, maybe fifty-five or so. He looked dangerous, somehow.

"I'm Lulu and this is my girlfriend Trixie, and you seem to have taken away our dates. What's up with that?"

"Lulu? What kind of a mother names her child Lulu?"

"Okay, it's Lucille, but I hate that name and Lulu has a little zest to it, doncha think? So, who's payin' this bar tab now that we've been dumped?"

"How'd you two girls like to go to a party this evening?"

"Hey mister, we ain't that kinda girls."

"You got me all wrong, Lulu. Christ, if I wanted hookers, I wouldn't be lookin for 'em in this place. No offense, no, I just need some pretty faces, and the rest of you two is also nice to look at. I might ask one of you, Lulu you seem to be the talkative one, to just talk to a guy. Maybe find out a little information. When it's all over I'll put you both in a cab and send you home. Whaddaya say?"

Lulu turned back to the bartender who hadn't gone far away. "Hey, bar guy! Is this guy legit? Are me and Trixie gonna end up in the river?"

"He's a good guy. Mr. Marcheti's nice to his friends. Course, you don't want to get on his bad side."

"Rock, thanks for the testimonial." Mr. Marcheti picked up the bar tab and handed it to the bartender. "Rock, take care of this, will ya?"

"You got it Mr. M.!"

The party was in the penthouse suite of a fancy hotel in the city. Some of the older women wore fancy gowns, but there were some girls Lulu and Trixie's age in the same short slinky dresses and open-toed spikes they wore. The men were older, more like Mr. Marcheti. They were all dressed in suits. Lulu and Trixie stayed together and just smiled at people without engaging in any conversation. They'd been there about half an hour when Mr. Marcheti took Lulu by the arm and pulled her into a corner on the far side of the room. "You see that guy over there talking to the bimbo in that red dress? I want you to go over, tell him your mother said to say hello."

"My mother?"

"Yeah. He'll think he knows who sent you and he'll ditch the bimbo and probably take you into a side room to talk. You just go with him and try to remember everything he says."

"What? What the hell is he going to tell me that's so important?"

"Don't worry, just listen for names and dates. I been watching you. You're smart. You haven't drunk anything or eaten anything since we got here. Your head's clear. You can do this."

Lulu crossed to the man talking to the girl in red, told him her mother had said to say hello and, as predicted, he took her arm gently, totally ignoring the other girl, and led Lulu down the hall. Before they had gone very far Lulu realized that someone was pulling on her other arm.

"Lu, darling, Lu, Lucille, honey, wake up."

"Oh, have I fallen asleep? I'm so awfully embarrassed. That was not very dignified of me. I hope I didn't snore. I feel such a fool. I think I was dreaming about another party. How absurd."

"Lucille, you're awake."

"Mother, I'm so embarrassed."

"Don't be my dear. There's someone who has been waiting all night to meet you. Tony Marcheti, this is my daughter, Lucille."

TRIXIE

They call me Trixie, but I don't do tricks. I'm not a hooker or a trained seal. It's Lt. Tracy Gomez, homicide division, Providence, Rhode Island. I don't know who started "Trixie" or why and now I don't care anymore. What's in a name? Somebody famous said that, right?

So anyway, this was the time I figured we were going to nail Slim Bonano. Slim, ha! He's five –six, maybe 275 lbs. What's in a name, I guess.

Slim was a small-time hood back when I was a rookie working the numbers runners in Cranston. That was back before the state took over the numbers racket. Now they call it "Lotto." So many times me and my sergeant had eye witnesses who were ready to testify that Slim was picking up betting slips, but the captain would always tell us, "No, I don't want the kids, I want the boss man." Me and the sergeant would head back out, knowing we weren't going to get anything on Jackie Nazarian. And even if we did, no one in the state of Rhode Island would dare walk into a court and testify against him. But you learn things as a rookie. You listen and you watch. And now I'm a lieutenant and Slim is the boss man and I was about to bust his fat ass.

Back in the day, Federal Hill in North Providence was Cosa Nostra territory. Now it's all fixed up as an Italian Heritage site with a dozen really excellent restaurants and even a couple of souvenir shops for tourists. You can buy a big bottle of coffee syrup and an autographed picture of former mayor Buddy Cianci.

Slim loved the new Federal Hill, especially the restaurants. He loved to tease the young waitresses with stories about the old days. "Sweetheart, when I was your age and this place was still a crummy bar I watched Rocky Maldone—he was a hood from Boston—get his head blown off right where you're standing. There was brains all over the floor. Ha! Now you can put that plate of spaghetti right here."

Marie's was one of the original restaurants on Federal Hill. Back in the 60s and 70s it was just a little bar with a couple of tables. On Sundays they'd close up and Marie Cardoza would put on a Sunday dinner for "her boys." People said that was her way of making her protection payments to the mob. After a while the place grew into an actual restaurant. Marie must have been one tough cookie. She never lost control of the business and now her daughter Regina and granddaughter Sharon are in charge. Slim was still a Sunday regular even though now the restaurant was open to the public on Sundays. He did enjoy talking to the young waitresses.

A lot of people thought he was just an old lech, but I've always thought he just missed having kids of his own and if somehow one of those nubile young things ended up in his bedroom he'd read her a story, tuck her in, and turn on the night light before he closed the door behind him. Or maybe that's just me thinking about kids I'll never have.

The crime scene was a mess. It was in one of the few old four-story walk-ups still standing out at the end of Atwells Avenue. The door on the fourth floor had been kicked in. The small cheap kitchen table had been knocked over, splashing the remains of a last meal across the small room. The well-worn linoleum floor was spattered with blood, while a large puddle still drained out of the victim. I picked up empty shell casings for my collection.

Raul St. Christopher, a mid-level drug dealer, had gotten way behind on his remittances to Slim. Slim had sent his two goons, Tony and Jonny, to rough Raul up a little. As they left him bleeding in a heap on that cheap linoleum floor he managed to call out, "Tell that fat bastard he'll get his money when I'm good and ready." This message was duly relayed to Slim at the tail-end of what had been a bad day at the end of a bad week. For one of the few times I'm aware of Slim Bonano must have just lost it. "No! That worthless piece of Puerto Rican dog waste does not talk to me that way! He's finished." And then Slim made his mistake, actually two mistakes, to be followed later by an even bigger one. First, instead of just sending Tony and Jonny to kill Raul and bury him in a sand pit out in Foster, Slim decided he personally was going to do the deed. His second mistake was using his favorite pistol, an old '.38 service revolver, which I'm pretty sure he had stolen from my sergeant back in the day. I had built up a bag of shell casings and actual slugs taken from crime scenes over the last twenty years. I knew if I could link Slim and that gun, he was going down, down, down. But I needed to put Slim and the gun together in front of witnesses. I was surprised the idiot had never dropped that old pistol in the Blackstone River, but for some reason he just couldn't part with it. For that I was thankful.

Maybe it was just because I was hungry, but later that day after finishing with the remains of Raul, I got the idea.

Angela Tribelli was twenty but she looked sixteen. She worked with us checking out package stores selling beer and cigarettes to minors. She was adorable. She had jet black hair falling halfway down her back and soft brown eyes. Her skin was a flawless shade of light olive and at just over five feet she was a little Italian doll. We spent the next week training her to be a waitress and she started work the following Sunday, at Marie's, at Slim's table.

"Good evening gentlemen my name is Angela and I'll be your server tonight."

"Whoa, whoa, whoa! Hey Sharon, this new girl—Angela right honey?"

"Yes sir."

"Yeah Sharon, this Angela, she's my waitress forever! You hear that? Forever."

"Would you like to hear tonight's specials?"

"Darlin' you are the special. And you don't have to write down a thing. Sharon knows what I want. You must be new here, right?"

"Yes sir."

"Jesus guys; they just keep getting younger and prettier. So, Angela, go get the bread and olive oil and tell Sharon to send over the first bottle of Chianti."

"Yes sir."

For the rest of the night Slim had something to say to Angela every time she came close to the table. Finally, near the end of the meal, when Slim was doing shots of grappa, I heard the words—of course she was wired, and every word was being legally recorded—I'd been praying for.

"So, Angela, you ever seen a real gun?"

"No sir, I haven't, except on TV and I don't know if those are real or not."

"You'll be here next Sunday, right?"

"I guess so, unless I get fired."

"Sharon fires you and she's gonna need a new line of work. Don't worry about that.

So, next Sunday maybe I'll have a little surprise to show you."

It could not have been prettier. Next Sunday, again when Slim was sipping his grappa, he called Angela over to his side of the table.

"Here you go honey. This is the real deal. Don't worry, there's no bullets in it. A guy named Raul needed 'em."

At which point I came out of the kitchen, Pete and Steve came from the front door, and Frank and Bill came from the back door.

"Slim Bonano I arrest you for the murder of Raul St. Christopher and a whole bunch of other crap. Allow me to read you your rights while the nice officers attach your handcuffs."

As some other famous guy said, "Thank heaven for little girls."

MULDOON

M uldoon retired from the police force with his full pension the day he reached fifty-five. He'd been a cop all his working life and he had had enough. He had always enjoyed the actual police work. It was the union bullshit and the precinct squabbles that made him crazy. If everyone would just focus on arresting the bad guys, things would have gone much smoother. And then, every few years the new mayor would make some pledge and things would get silly for a few months. Some mayors were all for cracking down on crime. So that meant the number of arrests had to go up, even if the number of crimes was actually going down. Then another mayor would be all for protecting everyone's civil rights. So then you practically had to have a judge's writ before you could even stop someone on the street, even if they were holding the murder weapon you'd been looking for. Crap and more crap. But he'd made it with only a couple of very minor bruises and one divorce. He had remarried and he and his wife were now looking forward to many years of travel and relaxing.

A week after Muldoon retired, they let Rafferty out on parole. Muldoon couldn't believe it. He had spent over a year gathering up enough evidence of chicken shit crimes to finally arrest Rafferty and put him in prison. It had always been impossible to make a case against Rafferty for the seven murders he had personally executed, the several drug operations he ran, or any of the other real crimes he had committed. Muldoon finally got him on rent control violations, a minor protection racket scheme, and enough other crap to put him in jail for five years. And then, after only two years, he got a "good behavior" parole. And of course the word on the street was that he was coming for Muldoon.

The funny part, I guess it was funny, was that Rafferty and Muldoon had been childhood friends. They grew up on the same block, went to the same elementary and high schools and were pretty close friends. But, as fate would have it, their paths diverged. Muldoon had an uncle who was a cop and Rafferty had an uncle in the mob. Muldoon graduated from high school and went into the police academy. Rafferty dropped out after tenth grade and went into the mob. Each of them did well and over the years moved up in their own ranks. Muldoon learned early on that going after Rafferty's crew was a job best left to the FBI. There was a kind of truce between the local cops and the local mob. Muldoon never liked the situation, but there was really nothing he could do about it. On the few occasions that he and Rafferty met each other they "made nice" and pretended that there was nothing wrong in the world.

As the years progressed Muldoon became more and more obsessed with Rafferty. A murder here, a serious bank robbery there; after a while it begins to bother you. And so, Muldoon started his campaign to get Rafferty on chicken shit. And it wasn't that hard. Rafferty was so used to committing major crimes that he ignored the little crimes and assumed everyone else also did. But not Muldoon. It took a long time, but finally

Muldoon was able to present the DA with a thick folder of minor crimes and evidence. At first the DA told Muldoon to forget it, but Muldoon was on a crusade. They brought the case to trial, and because all the charges were for apparently minor nonsense, Rafferty and his lawyers assumed the judge would dismiss everything and there would be no trial. There was a trial, and before Rafferty knew what had hit him, he was sentenced to five years. They sent him to a "white collar" prison with all the financial felons, which probably saved his life. And after two years his lawyers got him paroled.

When she heard about Rafferty's release Muldoon's wife wanted them to leave the country for a while. They'd wanted to travel and now seemed to be an excellent time to do that. Muldoon agreed that a long trip seemed like a great idea. But Muldoon had one thing to do before they left. Of course, it involved Rafferty.

Muldoon had used up all his minor crime evidence and now he was looking to put Rafferty away for good. It seemed fitting that they met in the old neighborhood. It was about a block from where the elementary school had been. Muldoon remembered that Rafferty used to spend time in a small Greek café there and he figured that was a good place to start looking. He was right. He walked in the door and looked around the room. There were people at some of the tables. One group of four men way in the back seemed very intent on a football fantasy league. And off to the side, his chair facing the door, there was Rafferty with a couple of his boys. "Well look what the wind blew in. Hello Muldoon. I think we have some things to discuss, you bastard."

"Ah, my dear friend Mr. Rafferty. How did you enjoy your two years in the country club? I assume you learned some new ways to steal money without using a weapon. Sorry, I had hoped you could stay there longer, but I guess they figured you had learned all you could learn and sent you home early."

"Okay Muldoon, how do we do this? Do you want me personally to put a bullet through you or shall I have my assistants do the job?"

"Rafferty, it has to be you. We can have a shootout like in the Old West. But let's step outside so we don't mess up your favorite hangout." Muldoon turned and walked towards the door. Rafferty pulled out a gun and shot him in the back. Muldoon lurched forward out the door and rolled to the side. The four men at the table in the back immediately rose, displaying guns and badges.

"Don't anybody move. Mr. Rafferty, I think premeditated attempted murder while on parole ought to get you a trip to a real prison. And, there are at least four witnesses."

"What do you mean attempted murder? I got Muldoon right in the back and I saw him go down." At which point Muldoon reentered the café.

"Rafferty, you got me. Just like I knew you would. Right in the back like the rat you are. I have to tell you, that Kevlar body armor is really amazing. I'm gonna need a new jacket and a new shirt and I think I'll have a black and blue mark for a while, but I'm going home, and you aren't. Goodbye Rafferty." And Muldoon again walked out the door.

DEATH ON RIDGE ROAD

I t was raining and cold that May day when I first met her. I hadn't slept much the night before. I was thinking about another dame that got away. My intercom buzzed and Charlene, my secretary, informed me that I had a client. Oh yeah, I'm a real private eye. Pete Max is the name and I don't leave the office without my gun. A grand a day plus expenses, and I'm worth it. Before she clicked off Charlene added, "Brace yourself boss. This one's a looker." That was just what I needed.

Honey Bordeaux was much more than a "looker." She was more of a stop dead in your tracks and stare and try not to drool while you stood there. She had long wavy blond hair, riveting sky blue eyes, and more curves than the big ride at Coney Island. Her dress, what there was of it, showed enough cleavage and upper leg to allow a pretty good medical exam. Maybe this was just what I needed after all. I shook her hand, checked out the gold and diamonds on each finger, and told her to take a seat. I buzzed Charlene that I didn't need to be disturbed for anything, including earthquakes, fires, and riots.

I told her to tell me her story and I hoped it was a real long one. It wasn't that long and it wasn't that new. Seems like Honey had got herself hooked up with Tony Strangetti, a local waterfront mob boss. Things had been going great until a couple of days ago when Tony disappeared, along with a hundred grand. The "boys" had been easy on Honey. No rough stuff at all. They just told her that if she planned to keep her pretty face and nice figure she better come up with Tony and the hundred grand. She had a week. Poor dame said she had no idea where Tony had gone or if he was even still alive. When she went into her crying routine it was all I could do to stay on my side of the desk and just pass her the Kleenex box. I told her not to worry. No one was going to hurt her and I'd ask around. Someone in this town knew where Strangetti was and why he'd taken the dough. I buzzed Charlene to come in and help Ms. Bordeaux out the back way and get her a cab if she needed one. I wasn't getting any closer to that broad than I absolutely had to.

So, I hit the bars and the pool halls. I even took a ride out to the track and lost twenty bucks on what had to be a sure thing. It was real strange. Everywhere I went people acted as if they had never heard of Tony Strangetti. That was like saying they'd never heard of the Statue of Liberty. Something was really wrong and I was heading right for the middle of it.

I was walking back from the track — that twenty had been my ride home — when a black sedan slowed next to me and the ugly mug of Nicki Pawlina emerged from the window, along with the muzzle of his .38. "Hey Petey. Get in the car; we'll give you a ride. Looks like your horse lost."

"Nicki, I don't usually accept rides from mobsters but since you asked so nice." And I climbed into the back seat, next to one of Nicki's gorillas. He even smelled like a real gorilla. "So Petey, let's have a little chat about our mutual friend Tony Strangetti. We saw his girlfriend goin' into your place yesterday. So what'd she have to say?"

"Sweet Ms. Bordeaux said you'd come around to see her. Said you told her that if she wanted to retain her pretty face she better come up with Tony, and quick. She also said Tony had taken a walk with a hundred grand."

"A hundred grand? It was more like four hundred grand! She told you we threatened her? That's pretty damn funny. We been lookin' for that dame ever since Tony disappeared. Yesterday was the first time we seen her, goin' into your place. And then it seemed like she never came out. She shacked up with you now?"

"I wish. No, I had my secretary take her out the back way and put her in a cab. I don't know where she went. If you ain't lyin' about not having seen her, it means she was lyin' to me. And Tony must have lied to her about the money. Man, you can't trust anyone these days."

"Yeah, Petey and why would she tell you that story?"

"Nicki, Nicki is there anything between those big ears of yours? Even I get it now. I fear our friend Tony was in love, and his heart wasn't the only thing that was throbbing. But he was afraid that sooner or later someone else, maybe even you Nicki, would try to take Honey away from him. So he decides to make a run for it. Of course, he takes a little cash to help him. Between them they come up with a plan to make you think Honey knows nothing about it. She wanted you to see her come to me. That was to make you think she really didn't know where Tony was. And she also wanted to make me think she didn't know where he was. She must have figured that you might come around for a little chat with me. Then, when we're all confused and looking in the wrong places, they slip out the back door together. Smart girl. But not smart enough. So you been watching Tony's office down by the water and that crappy hotel room he stays in, right?"

"Yeah, and we ain't seen either Tony or the broad."

"Nicki, Nicki, you're makin' me believe you never heard of Tony's little out of town bungalow where he stashes his girlfriends."

"What are you talkin' about? Where is it?"

"Tell your driver to get over to Route 101 and head north. I'll show you." The driver immediately cut across two lanes of traffic, ran a red light, and put us on 101 heading north, out of the city. After about ten miles I told them to turn off onto a little residential street. We drove less than a mile and I told him to stop and pull over. I could see Tony's little love nest about three houses down. I could also see another black sedan pulling out of the driveway and heading for us. "Everybody down!" I yelled and Tony, with Honey driving, cruised past us headed for 101. Nicki immediately screamed, "Get them bastards!" but I countered him with, "Not here, with all these houses around. Let's just follow them out of town. You can find a nice quiet spot and do what you gotta do." It occurred to me that if this played out the way it was heading, it would be another job I wouldn't get paid for.

It was already dusk as we drove out into the country onto a lonely stretch of 101 called Ridge Road. Nicki had had enough waiting. "All right, go get 'em." The driver stepped on it and soon we were only a couple of car lengths behind Honey's car. One of them must have recognized us and Honey floored it. She wasn't the greatest driver and she started to swerve from one side to the other. As we approached the top of the hill, we all saw a loaded eighteen-wheeler coming the other way. Honey yanked the wheel to the right, but the car's rear end let loose and she skidded sideways into the oncoming truck. Somehow

our driver managed to avoid the wreck and, just missing a tele-
phone pole, we crashed through three strands of wire fence,
taking four fence posts with us. We finally rolled to a stop about
twenty feet off the road. As we approached the mass of twisted
metal it was clear that Honey and the truck driver hadn't had
a chance. When we found Tony it was clear that he wouldn't
be running away with anybody or anything ever again. Nicki
climbed into the mess and emerged with a large briefcase. He
opened it to reveal stacks of hundred-dollar bills neatly wrapped
in packages of twenty. He grabbed one of those and threw it
to me. "Hey, Petey you might as well get paid. You found the
missing person." We jumped back in the car and were long gone
before the next vehicle came by and reported the wreck.

So now, when I can't sleep at night, I think of Honey
Bordeaux. It's better than counting sheep.

DR. BOB AND THE

OUTER SPACE ALIENS

I started reading in first grade and it has been a problem ever since. My house is now, of course, filled with books. I have purchased and built bookcases to fit in every available location and yet it is never enough. Part of my problem is the fact that I reread things. I know people who may read more than I do but who are happy to discard the latest best seller once they have completed it. I very seldom read best sellers. When I describe a book I may be reading or have recently finished I am usually greeted with a confused smile at best.

Part of the reason for my storage excess is the fact that I never discard a book I have enjoyed. I seldom discard a book I have not enjoyed.

Having reached the boundaries of book storage a few months ago I determined to dig into some of the oldest acquisitions and find a few feet of shelf space for the piles growing on the floor. Digging into my science fiction book case I came across a treasure. "Incredible Science Fiction Tales, Volume 13: Dr. Bob and the Outer Space Aliens." This title brought back memories.

I have failed to note that much of my early reading was in the form of comic books. I learned much history and literature from Classic Comics. And of course there was MAD Magazine for laughs. The science fiction comics were the best. Dr. Bob was always having adventures but this particular one led to my own adventure. It was because of an odd neighborhood man and his car.

I can't remember the man's name, if I ever knew it. But I remember him. He was a short, thin man who, whenever you might see him, wore a pale green jacket and a straw hat. He was odd and after a while we all, my friends and I, started calling him Dr. Bob after our favorite comic book character. It was the outer space aliens story that started it all. In that story the aliens had visited Dr. Bob and given him a strange machine. He was told to keep it until they returned. The same week that issue appeared we saw our Dr. Bob driving a very strange looking car. We were used to Fords and all the General Motors cars, but his machine was unlike anything we had ever seen. Years later I recall thinking that it might have been a Citroen. Of course, we immediately concluded this was the machine from the outer space aliens. We were determined to discover its secrets. Could it perhaps fly up into space? Could it become invisible? We determined to spy on the outer space machine and its owner.

The man lived alone and had no pets that we ever saw. He went off early in the morning and returned in the evening. This was exactly what our fathers did, but Dr. Bob did not drive his space machine. He was picked up and dropped off every day by a car driven by a woman and containing another woman who sat in the front seat. This in itself was very suspicious. None of our moms went to work. Who were these people and where were they all going? It was Jonny who remembered a story in

Volume 6. "Fire Maidens Attack" that told of alien women who came to Earth to steal boy children. Well, now that we knew what was going on, we had to inspect the alien machine.

The machine was kept in an old garage and taken out only on the occasional weekend when, now it made sense, Dr. Bob was sometimes seen driving around town with a woman in the passenger seat. All we had to do was get into the garage and take a close look at the machine. We would have to do it right after school, before he returned, and make sure not to disturb anything. We discussed the possibility that there might be an alien guarding the machine or perhaps a force field surrounding it. It was agreed that, for the safety of the Earth and boy children, we needed to find out what was in that garage.

Jonny and I were chosen to go first. If we did not return within half an hour, Steve would try to look in the window at the back of the garage and if Steve never came back, Randy would call the police.

It was a Wednesday afternoon and it must have been in late Fall because even now I remember that it was already starting to get dark by the time we got home and headed to Dr. Bob's house. Back then not all garages had roll up doors and his just had two large hinged doors that swung to each side to allow the machine to enter. Stealthily we went down his driveway and looked for any lights in the house that would indicate that he had come home early or that someone else was inside. Seeing nothing but still feeling uncertain, we approached the two tall garage doors and looked for a latch. There was only a large metal handle on one of the doors. We looked at each other realizing now was the time to attempt to enter or to turn tail and run. Jonny, after a quick glance in all directions, grabbed the handle and pulled. To the surprise of both of us the door easily swung open. We both blocked it from going too far, squeezed inside and shut the door behind us.

The machine sat in front of us clearly visible in the light coming through a back window. Up close it did look a lot like a car but was unlike any car we had ever seen. In an era of long sleek sedans with massive fins this thing, whatever it really was, was short and oval shaped. It was wider in front than in back and had only two doors. We had just finished a complete walk around when a man's not unfriendly voice asked, "Well boys, how do you like my machine?"

We both knew at that moment that we would shortly be on our way to planet Zagrad 7 with the rest of the boy children that had been captured. "I'd be glad to take you both for a ride, but the machine needs a special part that they are sending me. Once that's in you'll see how she just flies down the road." Today he was not wearing his green jacket, just an old brown bathrobe and house slippers. He was standing in the opening created when he had so silently pulled back one of the doors. How were we to escape? And then, for some reason, he held open the door and let us go. "Next time you come to visit please knock on the front door."

We ran up the driveway and across the street to where Steve and Randy were waiting and told them what had happened. There wasn't much to tell. Maybe it wasn't really an alien machine. We decided to just keep an eye on that garage and on our Dr. Bob. At least once each week one of us would sneak around to the back of the garage and peek in the window to see if the machine was still there. Once there was snow on the ground we had to stop since he would see our tracks. And after a while we sort of forgot about it. I don't remember ever seeing the machine on the road again.

The following Fall we entered Junior High and encountered the scariest, most mysterious creatures in the universe; Girls! Nothing in "Amazing Science Fiction Tales" had prepared us for this.

So, after recalling that childhood adventure there was no way I was about to discard any of those old volumes. I have now taken to just stacking new books under tables and chairs and looking for books belonging to my wife that she, now a Kindle reader, is willing to part with.

THAT FORK IN THE ROAD

O utside Conference Room #3 at the Marriott was a small table on which were arranged several rows of name tags. A printed sign stood at the back of the table stating, "Please take your tag, even if you choose not to wear it." Inside the room there were perhaps a dozen chairs arranged in a circle near the front of the room. A well-dressed man wearing a three-piece suit stood in back of one of the chairs and greeted people as they arrived. "Hello. I'm glad you were able to join us this afternoon. There are some modest refreshments on that table along the wall. Please, help yourselves."

One by one they arrived, saw the name tags, read the sign, and selected their tag. Most pinned them to an outer garment, a couple just put them in a pocket.

Alice Grey, a divorced recovering alcoholic, thirty-five and hoping to regain the custody of her daughter, had been sober for six months. She assumed this was the first of the out of town meetings that her new program had advertised. She knew she had made mistakes in her past, but was determined to get it right this time. She had been provided with a round trip plane ticket and a prepaid room in the Marriott. She was eager to find out what this step was all about. She thought briefly of pocketing her name tag, but then decided to be proud of herself for being here and pinned it onto the lapel of her jacket.

Thomas Abernathy, bank manager, lived an hour's drive away and had chosen to refuse the hotel room. He would be glad to get back to his wife and children when this sales booster meeting was over. He was still not sure of his role in sales. He knew the bank president had been trying to push new accounts and CDs, but that was not his job. Well, he would hear what they had to say, probably ignore it all, and go home having fulfilled his duty of showing up. He felt he had always made the right decisions in his life. He had a nice home and a nice family and an excellent job with all the benefits. Sometimes he wondered what might have happened if he had made a few different choices. How about a different college, a different major? What if, instead of marrying the first girl he fell in love with, he had played the field? What if he had never gotten married and become a suburban playboy? Well, none of those things had happened and he wasn't sorry.

Nancy Sullivan had been selling Tupperware for ten years and didn't need any more pep talks. The idea of a long weekend away from home, however, all expenses paid, was too tempting to resist. There had not actually been much of an explanation of what this meeting was about, but she didn't really care. A chance to spend time away from Stan and the girls was a welcome relief from the day to day grind. And she always flirted with the idea of what she might do if she encountered a nice-looking male Tupperware salesperson. Would she even dare? Last year in Ohio she had come very close, and ever since had regretted chickening out at the last minute. Looking around the room she didn't see anyone she thought was particularly attractive, but she did note that there were several men.

Olivia Jones was a chambermaid at the Marriott. She got the job after fleeing an impossible marriage and the town she grew up in. She had almost completed her associate degree in the community college when one day she just had to go. That was ten years ago. She had been at the Marriott for the last nine years and had been promoted to floor supervisor. Yesterday her boss had told her that "they" (whomever that was) wanted her to attend a meeting in Conference Room #3. She was to wear regular clothes, not her normal uniform, and was not to worry about being a chambermaid. She would, of course, get her regular pay for the day. Olivia thought this might be some sort of anti-union lecture. There had been a few organizers talking to the girls, but she had not been approached. She assumed that management was sending her to act as their spy.

Olivia had been among the first to arrive and wasn't sure if she should wear the name tag or not. She decided to just put it in her pocket.

Ralph Johnson was an unemployed factory worker from Mississippi. He denied being a racist but admitted that he didn't like "the blacks." He had been invited to this meeting, he was afraid, as part of his court ordered sensitivity training. He had gotten into a couple of shouting matches and had just avoided a fight by walking away from a large black man who had refused to get out of his way. Well, so far the only black face in the room belonged to a woman who had chosen not to wear her name tag. He wondered what she was so ashamed of that she wanted to hide her name. Typical, he thought. Well, she didn't really belong in this group anyway. Didn't those people have their own training groups?

Todd Ewing was a confused young man. When he was twelve he had decided that he must be gay. He was afraid of girls and just wanted to be with his best friend Randy. Randy, who had no doubts about his own desires, had tried to be physical with Todd, but Todd was too shy. Then, when he was sixteen, Todd had fallen passionately in love with Janice. With teenage hormones flooding both their bodies Todd had decided that he was not at all gay and he no longer was afraid of girls. But then Janice switched her love to Brad, a star member of the high school football team, and Todd decided to kill himself. Fortunately, the pills that he thought were his mother's anti-depression pills were only placebos that her doctor had "prescribed" for her. A bottle of sugar pills barely gave him a stomachache but, thinking he was about to die, he had called Janice and told her what he had done. Janice called 911 and the ensuing mayhem had led him to this meeting. Todd was ready to hear yet another boring lecture about how when you feel there is nothing left to live for, just dig down and REBOOT. As he looked around the room he realized that there were no other people his age. Were all these grownups also failures at suicide?

Dan Wentworth was a self-made millionaire. To hear him tell it, he had never made a bad decision in his life. He could pick the winners and he always had. He was married to a beautiful woman who had also done very well in her chosen career as a corporate lawyer. His only regret was his wife's decision to put off children until it was really too late. Perhaps if he had been a bit more forceful she might have changed her mind, but he felt that had been her decision. Aside from that he wouldn't change a thing. Not that he could of course.

"Mr. Wentworth, I believe you are the final member of our group. Please come in and shut the door behind you. There are still a few snacks on that table. Help yourself and then, everyone, please find a seat. I have put the chairs in a loose circle which I hope you won't find too intimate. I just don't like trying to be heard from a pulpit way in front of the room. When we are all settled I'll begin.

"Okay. I know each one of you thinks you know why you are at this meeting and I will tell you right up front, you're all wrong. Wait, before you panic, I'm not selling timeshares or anything else. I am here to offer you a possibly life changing opportunity. Again, no sales pitch is involved. Oh, and this is not a religious pitch either.

"I'm sure you all have an idea of what 'destiny' means and perhaps some of you have encountered the concept of 'predestination.' To an extent 'predestination' is true. You were all born with a predestined life path. In fact, everyone is born with a predestined life path. Before you ask, I have no idea how this happens or where these paths come from or if there is some big plan behind it all. I know there are some religions that believe in predestination, but I don't think their ideas are quite in line with what I am talking about.

"So, to cut to the chase, the reason you are here is, simply, that at some point in your life you have wandered off your predestined life path. I'll say that again. At some point you have wandered off your predestined life path. Before you ask, I have no idea when or how that happened. It could have been recently or long ago. 'Well,' you may be thinking, 'so what? Here I am and I can't go back.'

"It's true that you can't go back, but I am offering you a chance to return to your predestined life path. Okay, please hold the questions until I am finished. Then I'll answer whatever I can. If you choose to, you will be placed on your true life path and you will be living the life appropriate to that path. You will not be aware that anything has changed. You will be at the point in your life where you were meant to be at your present age. It could be vastly different from the life you now have, or it could be practically the same. Again, you will not be aware that you have not always been on your predestined life path. And, I must warn you, it is possible that your predestined life path would have caused your death before you had reached your current age.

"You will be given the opportunity to decide to stay as you are or return to your predestined life path. If you choose the predestined life path, sometime within the next twenty-four hours you will be there. You will be unaware that anything has happened, and life will go on. Obviously if you choose to remain as you are, nothing will happen, and you will continue your life as you were. You won't, however, remember this meeting. You will remember attending a very uneventful meeting of the type that you walked into this room expecting. And you won't remember seeing any of the other people in this room.

"Okay, I'll try to answer questions. No, this is not a matter of good or evil. You have not strayed from some holy or righteous path you were supposed to have followed. You did not make a bad choice. You just made the wrong choice.

"Who cares and why are we being offered this opportunity? I have no idea. I am here because that seems to be my job. As you may have guessed, I'm not from around here. You were chosen and got your invitations and plane tickets and hotel rooms from someone or something I don't understand. When I leave this meeting I will soon find myself in another room with another group.

"How are you supposed to know which decision took you off the path? There is no way to know. I would suggest that you don't try. Remember this is not a matter of good vs. evil.

"Is there some sort of punishment if we don't return to our predestined path? Not that I'm aware of. And there is no prize for deciding to return, unless you think your life could not be worse, I suppose. But, please, don't take that to mean that your life will improve if you do return to the path. It might get much worse.

"So, here's the way this is going to work. You won't be going out the doors you came in. Those doors are locked. You will be going out the door at the front of the room. Please go one at a time. You will enter a smaller meeting room where you will find two boxes on a table. One is labeled RETURN TO PATH, the other is labeled STAY AS I AM. If you wish to return to the path just put your name tag into the RETURN box. If you wish to remain as you are you can put your name tag in the STAY box, or just keep it as a souvenir of this odd meeting. When you leave that room, please close the exit door behind you. That will let this door open to allow the next person to enter. That's really all I have to say. Oh, grab another snack before you go if you'd like. Thank you for your attention."

HOWARD

Howard thought things would be better for him after Sandra moved out and went to live with that used tire salesman, Arnold. What the heck were used tires? Is that what they used to call retreads? He could imagine Arnold pitching them to some poor bastard who didn't have enough money to even own a decent car and needed new tires for the heap he was driving. "Sir, the modern steel belted radial tire is virtually indestructible. Only the tread itself wears away. With our patented Vulcan-Plus process we rebuild the treads to their factory new condition, and you get a tire that is equivalent to brand new for a fraction of the cost of new." What a crock that was! And what did Sandra see in that guy anyway? She was always saying that Howard wasn't spiritual enough. What did that mean? Was Arnold spiritual? Arnold, that lying son of a bitch, spiritual? Maybe he was just better in bed. Thinking about that idea made Howard feel sad. What else should he have done? What things did Sandra and Arnold do? God, there were only so many ways you could fit two bodies together, and he was pretty sure they had tried them all. Did being spiritual have something to do with it? How could it? Wasn't being spiritual supposed to be like being holy? And all the holy people, priests and nuns, weren't supposed to have anything to do with sex. Howard didn't understand. Maybe he could just forget about Sandra. Yeah, and maybe he'd win the lotto.

Howard swung around on his bar stool and looked at the woman sitting next to him. She was probably about forty, pretty nicely put together, wearing a blue dress with a low neckline showing some attractive cleavage. He couldn't recall if she had been there when he had sat down an hour and three Jack Daniels ago. She didn't seem to be with anyone. Was she a hooker? She didn't have any rings on her left-hand ring finger, but she had a gold thumb ring on her right hand and a simple silver band on the index finger of her left hand. Jesus, was that some lesbian code or something? He needed to ask her a question. What could she do, tell him to get lost? That wouldn't hurt as much as Sandra leaving. How do you start; "Miss," or "Miz," or just start talking? That sounded the simplest. He looked at her for a while until he was pretty sure she knew he was watching and then he spoke.

"So, what does it mean to be spiritual? It doesn't make any sense to me."

"As long as the word 'Jesus' doesn't come out of your mouth, we can talk about this. It looks like we both need another drink. Hey, Larry! We need some refills over here."

She swung her stool a little bit in Howard's direction but waited for the drinks to arrive before she spoke. Somehow he knew enough to keep quiet.

"Now, are we talking about that New Age crystal and pyramid crap or one of the major religions here? Not that it matters, but my name is Helen."

"Oh, I'm Howard. Why doesn't it matter?"

"What? Oh, well I don't think we'll see each other again

after we solve your philosophical problem is all. So what is it, crystals or the Pope? Shit, I hate drinking this stuff, but it does make it easier to talk to strangers and since I don't know anyone but the bartender..."

They were actually staring into each other's eyes at this point, but then Howard looked down only to realize he was staring at her cleavage. He looked back up into her eyes.

"Very good. My eyes are up here. You know it's your turn to talk now."

"Right, sorry. Okay, my girlfriend, well I guess she's my ex-girlfriend now, says I'm not spiritual enough and I don't have any idea what she is talking about."

"Howard, right? Howard, if she is your ex-girlfriend why do you give a shit what she thinks? You planning to try to win her back? I'm guessing if you have spirituality differences it ain't gonna happen."

"No, that's not it. She's with Arnold now. I just want to know what she was talking about. I realized I have heard people talking about being spiritual, but I have never had any idea what they meant by that. I don't think it means that they go to church every Sunday. I guess it might mean they believe in god, but I also think it might mean they believe in something other than the regular god that they tell you about in church. But I don't mean crystals and pyramids. Is it some kind of magic?"

"You really are serious. I gotta admit, I thought that was the best pick-up routine I had heard in six months. But I'm not looking to get picked up, just so we're clear on that."

"I am serious, and how do I say I wasn't trying to pick you up without it sounding like an insult? I mean, well you're good looking and..."

"Okay stop. No picking up, no insult taken. Let's get back

to spirituality. I just think it means you believe there is more than just the everyday world we deal with every day. It's the place where dreams come from. It's a belief that there is something bigger than us."

"But that all sounds like bullshit to me. All the gods and religions are just ways to believe in and try to invoke magic powers. And I don't believe in magic. And all that about how magical and illogical quantum mechanics seems to be is just nonsense too. Just because we haven't got a rational clue as to how the world works doesn't mean it is irrational."

"What are you, some kind of scientist? Quantum mechanics, rational and irrational? You just left my comfort zone. But I happen to agree with you that magic, real magic, not magician's tricks, seems very unlikely. But I'm also coming to the conclusion that I don't really know what people mean by spiritual either. And before we started this I would have said that I did. I guess I can't help you. Sorry."

Helen swung her stool back towards the bar, slid off it, picked up her purse, and walked away. I waved to the bartender. He came over and I said "So I guess I'm paying for my drinks and whatever the lady had."

"Which lady would that be?"

"The one in blue that was sitting next to me?"

"Sorry, I must have missed her. All I have is the four Jacks on the rocks for you."

"And I suppose your name isn't Larry?"

"No, sorry, I'm Bruno. But, you know, that's funny. A couple of nights ago someone else asked me if my name was Larry."

SMALL VIOLIN

T hey were eating dinner at one of those darling little restaurants on the upper east side of Manhattan when Winston put down his fork, looked across the table at his wife Brenda, and said, "I'm done." Brenda looked down at his plate and, still holding her fork in the air, replied, "But you haven't even started eating."

He looked off to his left, at nothing in particular, and said, "No I don't mean with dinner, I mean with this whole deal. We're both in our fifties. We have been working steadily since we finished school and we have amassed a pile of money. We never got around to having children, but we have traveled all over the world. God, we've seen the pyramids, Machu Picchu, the temples of Angkor Wat and whatever else there is to see. We have a big apartment right on Central Park, and I have just had enough of it all."

Brenda, who had lowered her fork to her plate, looked across the table for a short while and then spoke. "Wow! Where did that come from? I thought you loved going into the financial wars every day and coming home with more bags of money each night."

"And do you still love making those big corporate real

estate deals and coming home with bags of commission dollars every night?" And now it was Brenda who quietly stared off into nowhere.

"You know, I don't anymore. It's just what I do." And then they were both silent for a while. Brenda broke the silence. "So, what do we do? Have you been thinking about this for a long time?"

"No. It just came to me. I realized that somehow, we forgot the whole family thing with kids and grandchildren and the big family dinners. Don't worry, I'm not suggesting we run out and adopt a bunch of orphans. I just want to... I don't know what I want. What's the opposite of the lives we have right now?"

"Starving on the streets of Delhi?"

"Okay, good point, not that opposite." Winston picked up his fork and started eating. "We've got some thinking to do," he said, picking up his wine glass.

It took them several months to untangle themselves from their jobs and to find the abandoned fifty-acre dairy farm in Vermont. It took another six months to take apart the barn and use many of the beautiful wide oak planks as part of a new farmhouse which was carefully constructed to resemble an early nineteenth century Vermont farmhouse. They sold their apartment overlooking Central Park for enough money to cover the land and the new house in Vermont—not that money would ever be a problem. The monetary symmetry just seemed to enforce the feeling of trading one lifestyle for something completely different.

It was spring when they moved to Vermont. They had been all set to buy a big Range Rover, but at the last minute decided that if they were going to ever be accepted by the neighbors they should chose a Subaru Outback, which they did. They wanted to become part of the small community. They got library cards, went to town meetings, and ate many meals in the two little restaurants. When asked what they planned to do when their acres were ready for haying, they readily agreed to allow the Hanscom brothers to continue cutting those fields as they had been doing for the last ten years. It was agreed that no money needed to change hands. Winston and Brenda wouldn't charge for the hay and the Hanscoms wouldn't charge for "mowing the lawn."

It was two weeks before haying was to begin that they first heard it. The sound was that of a violin being played very softly, almost as if by a child. They searched the house for a radio or unattended laptop, but couldn't find the source of the music. It was Brenda who realized it was coming from outside, but it was Winston who saw her first. She was a small blond girl wearing what could have been a decorated deerskin coat, softly playing a small violin. The grass came up above her waist, but she was standing in a path that seemed to lead back into the fields. She was looking down at her instrument and appeared to be unaware that she now had an audience. She finished playing and, still looking down, turned and started to walk away along the path back into the fields. Before Winston or Brenda could speak, she just disappeared.

It was Brenda who spoke first. "Tell me we both saw a little girl playing a little violin and then she disappeared. Or have I lost it entirely?"

"No. I saw her and heard the violin and watched her disappear. It's as if this place is haunted. I hope someone in town can explain what just happened."

It was the old librarian, Mrs. Reed, who knew the story. "Oh yes. That was Caroline Jenkins you saw. Years ago the entire

Jenkins family died in the fire that completely destroyed the farm house. Caroline was the only one pulled from the flames and she lay in the hospital for a week before she finally passed. For the first few years after the fire, Caroline would appear just before haying began. When I saw that you had rebuilt the old house and even used some of the wood from the barn I wondered if we might see her again. We haven't seen her for a long time. It's good to have her back."

BALLOUVILLE

I was traveling east, from Hartford, Connecticut to Providence, Rhode Island along Route 44, long before the highway was built, when I missed a turn south of the town of Pomfret and became lost in an area of small roads and lonely villages. It was late October and being well after noon the sun had already begun to settle in the west. I decided to abandon my goal of reaching Providence that day and, instead, began searching for lodgings for the night. Having passed no public buildings, I stopped in front of a large brick edifice which, being next to a rapidly coursing river, I concluded must be a mill of some sort. I left my automobile and approached the door to what I assumed was the mill office. There was a light shining through a window, and I hoped this indicated that there was someone inside who might provide me with directions to an inn or even a rooming house that could accommodate me for the night. I anxiously knocked on the heavy wooden door which contained a large brass plate announcing "Ballou Mill." There being no immediate response I knocked again. As there was no reply to my second attempt, I decided to try the door, which proving to be unlocked, I opened. Rather than entering I leaned slightly into the room and yelled. "Hello! Is there anyone here?"

I stood motionless, straining to hear any response when

suddenly, as if from nowhere, there was a large hand clamped onto my shoulder and the words, "Who the hell are you and what do you want?" resounded. I turned around to face my adversary and found, much to my surprise, a large woman dressed in machinist's coveralls staring down at me. She had dropped her hand from my shoulder as I turned and, again to my surprise, appeared to be smiling. Before I could say a word, the woman spoke. "I'm sorry. You're not at all who I thought you were. We've been having trouble with some travelers. But who are you anyway?"

I gave my name and explained that I was just looking for assistance in finding a place for the night. I told her that I was trying to get to Providence but had lost my way. She thought for a short time, and then slowly shaking her head said, "You'd have to go back to Pomfret to find any place to stay, and I expect you'd get lost trying to do that. You'd better come home with me. Just let me finish closing up." Having spoken she moved past me into the office, turned off the light, came back out, and locked the door. Again, she spoke. "I guess that's your car. You can give me a ride home." Without further words she strode to my car, opened the passenger side door, and carefully lowered her large frame onto the seat. I took my seat, started the engine, and asked "Where to?" Her reply was, at the time, slightly strange. She seemed to ponder the question, as if there could be more than one answer to where she lived. At last, nodding her head, as if having made up her mind she said, "Just keep driving along this road. I'll tell you when to turn." As I drove, I began to wonder how she had planned to get home if I had not come along. There had been no other automobiles near the mill, and we had already driven more than a mile when she indicated that I should turn onto a narrow dirt lane that veered to the right off the main road. By this time, it had become dark enough for me to turn on my headlights. Because of the darkness and the narrowness of the road I had to greatly reduce my speed. The road started downhill and soon we came alongside the river and approached a small brown shingled house.

"This is it. Just stop by that tree. Wait in the car until I tell you to come in." And with that enigmatic phrase she left the car and walked slowly towards the building. Watching her go I realized that she must be well over six feet tall and must weigh twice what I weighed. She appeared to unlock the side door and entered the house. There was suddenly a loud baying as if from a very large dog and as I listened, I became aware of two dogs, both of similar voice. Suddenly the door opened and out came the two mastiffs, barking and bounding directly towards me. The woman appeared in the doorway and called to me. "You can come in now. I told them you're company." This did not at all reassure me, but I noted that the dogs' tails were wagging and that instead of growling they were happily, I hoped, barking. I slowly opened the car's door and stepped out, prepared to dive back into my car if either of the large dogs became aggressive. They were content to thoroughly sniff me and, apparently satisfied that I posed no threat to them or their mistress, they backed off slightly. With only the light from the open house door to guide my way, I walked to the house with a dog on either side and entered.

I was surprised to find myself in a small kitchen in front of a table on which a modest meal had been laid. The woman instructed me to sit down and eat and indicated that she had already had her evening meal. Somewhat hesitantly, noting that the two dogs had retreated to the far corners of the room, I sat, thanked her for the hospitality, and ate. I remember nothing about what I ate. I think there was a glass of warm beer as a beverage. Following my dinner my hostess said there was a small room above the kitchen in which there was a cot and a blanket which I could use for the night. She dealt with the dishes and then excused herself, saying she had chores, and accompanied by the dogs opened the door and went out.

Although it was still early, darkness had come and, finding myself unaccountably tired, I went upstairs, found the room with its cot and blanket and settled down for the night. I must have fallen immediately to sleep, and it was the sound of the kitchen door opening and then softly shutting that awoke me the next morning. I arose, folded the blanket, and proceeded downstairs. As I entered the kitchen expecting to encounter my hostess from the previous evening, I was taken aback to see a much smaller and younger woman sitting in one of the kitchen chairs holding a rifle which was pointed directly at me. She spoke, almost as if she were reciting a line in a theatrical production. "Who the hell are you and what do you want?"

I started to reply "But that's exactly…"

She finished what I was going to say. "Exactly what she said." With that she put the gun on the floor and appeared to relax. "Sorry about the gun. I was just making sure. It's All Hallows' Eve and she's managed to do it again. Did she find you at the old mill? And she invited you here, and those two dogs came out and gave you the once over? And I'll bet you are really hungry this morning even though she fed you last night?"

I was slow to gather my wits about me, but I finally managed to reply. "Why yes, everything you just said is exactly what happened. And I am famished. Please explain what is going on, and where are that woman and her dogs?"

Her answer was not at all what I had expected. "It'd be hard to say where they are. The three of them were murdered on this night ten years ago by a passing stranger and every year she comes looking for him. I often wonder what will happen if he ever does come back."

DARLENE

Hi! I'm Patti. I remember the first time I saw Darlene. It was our junior year of high school. I guess it was the cascades of soft red curls that framed her face and reached below her shoulders that impressed me the most. But as she came closer I realized she had eyes that I can only describe as electric blue. Her pixie nose was the center of a field of reddish brown freckles which appeared perfectly positioned on her pale white skin. Hers was the most striking face I had ever seen. And she was just barely five feet tall—a perfect little doll.

My immediate response was to see her as a rival. No boy in the school was going to look at me if Darlene was anywhere in sight. And then she opened that beautiful pink rimmed mouth and the saddest voice I had ever heard asked if I would walk with her to lunch. She was afraid of the two boys that had been following her all morning between classes. I looked and saw Ty and one of his soccer buddies almost drooling as they stared at Darlene. I would have laughed out loud at those two idiots, but I could see that Darlene really was spooked by their attention. Instead I took her arm as if we were old friends and steered her down the long, noisy hall towards the cafeteria.

It was early in the school year, the first week of September, and still pretty warm. I was, of course, wearing the shortest skirt the dress code would allow, a totally cute top, and some little heels to push my butt out. I was Little Miss Hot Stuff, right? Darlene was dressed as if she had picked her clothes out of the Goodwill's rejects. I knew about dressing to avoid attention — a dumb idea, I thought — but this was ridiculous. She had on a baggy brown sweater over some hideous green boys' cargo pants and wore dirty pink sneakers. Some inner angel of mercy allowed me to keep my big yap shut about her fashion choices right then.

We ate lunch together that day and then almost every day for the rest of the year. That first day I realized that Darlene had not brought anything to eat and didn't appear to have any money to buy anything from the lunch ladies. I almost had to cram it down her throat, but I did get her to eat half of my turkey sandwich and half of the apple Mom had also packed. I bought a bottle of water and convinced her that I was just going to throw the second half away, so she may as well have it. She thanked me and drank it down. That afternoon I told my mom about Darlene and asked her to pack a double lunch for the rest of the week. She agreed to that, but she also got on the phone with the school office and got Darlene set up for free lunch starting the next week. I guess the school already knew something about Darlene. My mom was wonderful.

Darlene didn't talk much that first day. She thanked me for getting her away from the boys, asked my name and where I lived, and that was about it. When I asked about her, she was almost reluctant to admit that she lived on the second floor of the one house in town that had been divided into two separate units. It was in the older end of our town. It wasn't run down

ROBERT C. GWIN, III

or anything, just kind of old and a little sad. The house had one of those big wrap around porches, but nobody ever sat outside anymore. The paint wasn't peeling but it just looked drab. The bushes need trimming and the little bit of front lawn was always covered with leaves and twigs. I picked up pretty quickly that her family didn't have much money and realized that her choice of clothes was not a fashion statement. It was an unintended economic statement. As the first week of school progressed, it turned out that Darlene and I were in three classes together. She was in advanced algebra though. It turned out she was pretty smart. If I ever made it through introduction to algebra it was going to be front page news.

It took a month before I could talk Darlene into coming back to my house after school. I think she was just very shy and, I guess, a little ashamed of not having any money. Mom and my little sister are so great! They were all over Darlene as if she was our long lost sister. After the first ten minutes in my house I saw the first really big beautiful smile on that adorable face. It took a lot of negotiations and my mom offering to call her father before Darlene agreed that maybe she could stay for dinner. She didn't let Mom call, though. She called and talked, so quietly I was unable to eavesdrop, to someone and then announced that it would be okay. When Dad got home Darlene went back into her shy mode and almost seemed to want to stay close to me. I never thought he was that scary, but my dad was a tall man. He was also pretty smart and realized that Darlene was a little unsure of him. Instead of coming on all hardy and cheerful he just said, "Hello Darlene, glad to finally meet you. Patti talks about you all the time." And then he pretty much ignored her for the rest of the night. It must have worked perfectly because while we were walking back to her house she said, "Your dad's really nice," and sounded a little surprised. When we got to her house I was sort of hoping she'd let me come in and meet her family, but she just said, "Thanks for dinner. See you tomorrow," and ran up the steps, unlocked the door, and went inside. It was a warm night and just getting dark and I was really tempted to stay near her house and see if I could see anyone inside as they turned on the lights. But then that just seemed a little creepy so I jogged back home.

When I finally did get inside Darlene's house it was not what you'd call enjoyable. One day at the end of our last class, English I think, Darlene said, "Hey, can you come back to my house for a minute? I want to show you something." Well, she didn't have to ask me twice. I had been waiting for this for the last couple of months.

It was about a ten minute walk to Darlene's house and although I asked several times what she was going to show me, she wasn't telling. When we got there she looked up and down the street. I think she was checking to see what cars were parked, or actually, to make sure a certain car wasn't parked there. We went up the front steps and she unlocked the outer door. Then we went up the inner staircase and she unlocked the door into her part of the house. As soon as she was inside she yelled, "Ryan, are you here?" There was no answer, but she held me at the door for almost a minute listening for any sounds. Finally she told me to follow her and we walked down a poorly lit, bare hallway to her room. There were no decorations or pictures on either side of the hall and the old rug on the floor just looked tired. I was pretty surprised when she picked another key off her ring and unlocked the door to her room.

It's strange as I think about it now, but watching her unlock her room seemed just wonderful to me then. Wow! Can you imagine me asking my mother if I could lock her out of my room? Are you serious? It wasn't until sometime later that I realized what that locked door really represented and why that lock needed to be there. And then I wanted to cry. But on that occasion I was just amazed at what I took to be Darlene's great independence. And what did she want to show me? New clothes! She had finally convinced her father that high school girls dressed differently than adolescent boys and he had actually given her a clothes allowance. It wasn't much, but she had done pretty well with it. Of course it was all tops and pants. Darlene didn't ever wear a dress or a skirt the entire time she was in high school. But at least she now had a little color in her wardrobe. And, once again, my guardian angel stopped me before I could utter one negative word about style or color choice. I was wise enough to simply gush, "Darlene, they are beautiful!" I really wasn't expecting what happened next. She threw her arms around my neck and kissed me right on the lips. And then she started crying as if her heart was broken. I just put my arms around her and held her for the next few minutes.

And then she looked up at me and said, "Patti, I love you, not in some romantic icky way, I just love you. And you are the only person in my life that I love. Please say it's okay. You don't have to love me back. Just let me love you."

Before I could recover enough to put together a response, there was the sound of the front door banging open and I heard a male voice yell, "Hey, Darlene! You home yet? What's for dinner, anyway?"

Darlene's tears stopped immediately and she stepped away from me and spoke softly. "Shit! Don't worry. That's just my half-brother Ryan. He's really loud and tries to act all scary, but he's just a stupid jerk. And in case there is any doubt in your mind, I hate him. He thinks he can boss me around, but if he gets too bad my father beats the crap out of him. I was hoping you wouldn't have to meet him. You probably ought to go now."

Again the voice yelled, now from just outside her door. "Hey, why's your damn door locked? What the hell are you doing in there?"

And now it was time for Darlene to yell back. "Ryan, Dad came home early and we were talking about sending you back to jail."

After a short pause, during which I guess Ryan was trying to figure out if Darlene was telling the truth, he replied, in a voice that was now much less sure than it had been, "You liar! He ain't home. His car's not outside. Are you coming out?"

Darlene's reply was in the strongest and most self-assured tone I had ever heard from her. "Ryan, I'm coming out there and I have my best friend Patti with me. If you even look at her I'll tell Dad to beat the living shit out of you and you know he'll do it. Go sit in the kitchen."

And then, softly now, to me, "Are you ready? Remember, he doesn't bite, he just barks a lot."

I felt myself torn between wanting to defend Darlene and wanting to get as far away as I could. But suddenly the shy little Darlene had apparently become a firm, self-assured young lady. She unlocked her door and led me out to meet the monster.

Ryan was no longer standing just outside Darlene's door. He was in the kitchen, sitting at the small table, looking down at the floor. As I passed by he never even slightly lifted his head and didn't seem to acknowledge my existence. What had happened? What was the weird family dynamic that had suddenly turned things around? Now I really wanted to be back in my totally normal, no locks on my bedroom door, home. Patti looked at me with those piercing blue eyes and said "Remember what I said, please?" I just nodded and sort of backed out the door, somehow made it down the stairs and the front steps, and sprinted all the way home. And that was my introduction to Darlene's family life.

If anyone ever needed someone to love it was Darlene. And I realized, after the initial shock, that all she wanted was a sister. And I knew all about loving my sister so adding another sister was no problem at all. Darlene and I became very close. I never did meet her father and I only saw Ryan a couple of times after that first encounter. Both times he acted as if looking at me would turn him to a pillar of salt. I was dating a bunch of guys at that point and I tried to get Darlene to go out with someone, but she just couldn't do it. And here is where the great rumor about Darlene, Ty, and I got started.

I really liked Ty and most certainly not as a brother. Well Ty and all the other boys were just totally fascinated by Darlene and the fact that she wouldn't even go to McDonalds with any of them. So, I wanted to go out with Ty and I realized that Darlene had never been on a date, so I had one of my all-time dumb ideas. This was senior year and I was still trying to pass introduction to algebra, just so you know how well my brain was working. Anyway, I concocted the brilliant idea that all three of us—Ty, Darlene, and I—would go out together. I didn't think Darlene would go along with it, but I was sure Ty would think it was the greatest idea I had ever had. He was also flunking introduction to algebra for the third time. To my great surprise Darlene agreed. And where did we all decide to go? Again, pure brilliance on my part; The Prairie View drive-in. Ty thought he had won the lottery and started bragging to all his buddies about what was going to happen. Wasn't he King Rooster? So what really happened that night? Well, I must admit that I did spend most of the movie playing kissy face with Ty and fending off his hands. But then Darlene said it was pretty boring in the back seat all alone and when were we going home? Ty invited her to join us in the front but, since his mother's car had bucket seats in the front but not in the back, we all climbed into the back. I was in the middle. Ty was the instigator of what happened next. He leaned over and kissed me so I kissed him back, but then he leaned back and said "Now, Patti you kiss Darlene. Just do it. Darlene doesn't want to kiss me, but she'll let you kiss her, won't you?"

"Sure, okay."

Well that was a pretty silly night at the drive-in. There was no more problem with roving hands and I only opened my mouth when I kissed Ty. After about ten minutes we all started laughing and couldn't stop. And that was the end of that, we thought. We didn't know that because of all Ty's bragging there were about a dozen cars around us watching our every move. When we all climbed into the back seat they assumed it must be a three way orgy and that was the story that swept through school on Monday. Ty didn't know whether he should tell the truth or take credit for the greatest event in Prairie View's history. So he responded with, "What, do you really believe that?" and then he would wink. That boy just couldn't get over himself.

I thought Darlene would be humiliated and very upset with me but that was not the case. "Patti, guess what? The girls have stopped calling me a lesbo. Now they just call me 'you slut!' I think that's an improvement don't you?" And we both started laughing. A few weeks later there actually was a repeat, but it was very different, in spite of what everyone said. I really wanted to see the movie and I figured why not let Ty pay for it. Darlene and I sat in the back seat and Ty sat in the front, all alone, trying to convince me to join him or to at least let him come into the back seat. And Darlene and I weren't making out either. We were laughing at Ty.

We all graduated from high school that spring and I actually got into junior college as a fashion major. Ty went to California to grow grapes or something like that. Darlene, who was smarter than Ty and I put together, took a horrible job in a meat packing plant. The pay was good, which is why she took it, but the smell around that place was enough to make me want to swim through a vat of Clorox. I mean yuck. I visited her a couple times that first year when I came home for Thanksgiving and Christmas. She didn't seem happy. We exchanged a couple of letters, but I felt guilty telling her all about my fun life when she was having no fun at all.

And then it was time for spring break ("Mom can I have $2,500 to go to Florida and get drunk and have sex with strangers?" What do you think?); of course I went home. But when I went to look for her, there was no one at her house and it turned out that Darlene had left her job and moved away with her father and stepbrother. I was both hurt and worried that she hadn't even sent me a card telling me where she had gone. And the more I thought about her the more worried I got. I asked all around town and even went out to that horrible meat packing plant. Everyone said the same thing, she was here one day and gone the next. I didn't know where her father had worked or Ryan, if he actually had a job. So I went back to fashion school and waited.

Well I guess the dog finally decided to bite back. It was

big news. I cried for a long time when I read it in the paper: "Enraged Son Shoots and Kills Father and Stepsister and Then Himself." I can only guess that his father beat him one too many times and poor Ryan finally lost control. The details of the story indicated that it appeared Darlene had died trying to stop Ryan from shooting her father. They hadn't actually moved very far away and I'll never know why they moved or why Darlene never sent me a letter. I worry that maybe she did write but it got lost, and when I didn't reply she just assumed, in her sad little way, that I had forgotten her.

I'll always wonder what I could have done that would have kept Darlene alive. What if I had not gone away to college and stayed around? Then, maybe, we could have moved to some-place far away from here and shared an apartment and found jobs. Heck, we could have found husbands and had a double wedding. But I left her in that mess to go off to fashion school. And I'll always believe that I was the only person she ever really loved.

BENEFIT

Where to begin the tale that has led me here? I suppose at the beginning, if that truly was the beginning. This is what I remember.

Thinking to improve my lot in life, I had recently entered the real estate business and, on that day, was in an unfamiliar city with a new client.

This client was an older man who, even on this warm day, wore a long dark coat which reached almost to his old but well-polished black shoes. He was slightly taller than I, with wide shoulders and long arms. His face too was long and had dark bushy eyebrows which extended upwards above his sunken eyes and large nose. His thin lips appeared to be pinched shut, but when he spoke his mouth opened wide and emitted an odd kind of loud hoarse whisper. I noticed also that his hands, which looked old with well pronounced veins, had slim fingers with perfectly trimmed nails. They were the hands of a thinker, not of a laborer. He wore no hat, but his head was well covered with thick black hair parted on one side and shiny with mildly fragrant hair oil.

It had been raining heavily earlier in the day, but when we arrived the deluge had ended. The clouds were breaking up and the afternoon sun was peeking through; a late August day in

New England. Benefit Street is one of the older streets in Providence, Rhode Island, the third street uphill on the east side of the Moshassuck River. Along the historic street are houses from the early nineteenth century and a few from a century before. My client and I were making our way up the winding stone steps of one of the oldest houses on the street.

In spite of the emerging sunshine, the house remained strangely shaded by the few remaining clouds and the tall oak trees beside it. Its brick walls were thickly covered with ivy, which had by now started to cover some of the lower windows. The house was set into the hillside and the back side was, in fact, partially contained by the slope.

As we ascended the steps, I spoke over my shoulder to my client who followed slowly. "This property hasn't been shown in over a year. I apologize if it's a little dusty inside. I'm told that the last people to look at it were from the Arkham Historical Society. According to my office they said that after inspecting it thoroughly they had concluded that, in their words, 'This is the one.' But then the office never heard from them again." My client, who as noted was much older than I and more subdued in dress and attitude, nodded his head but did not otherwise respond.

I struggled for a bit but finally got the old lock to open, and with a firm twist on the worn brass knob and an almost violent shove on the heavy wooden door, I managed to enter the old house. My client, who, apparently while I was working to open the door had put on a heavy paper dust mask, followed me in and switched on a large battery powered lantern with which he quickly swept the darkened room. The few remaining pieces of antique furniture, picked out by the light of the darting lantern, were protected by greying dust covered sheets. Heavy drapes concealed the tall narrow windows. I slowly pulled back one of the drapes releasing a shower of dust particles which took on an unpleasant yellowish hue in the faint slanting beams of the afternoon sun. The sunlight was barely able to penetrate the dirt covered ancient panes of glass and did little to illuminate the gloomy room. The air had an aroma of old mold and an undefinable sourness. I recall coughing from the dust, then, working to clear my throat, I addressed the client.

"Well, where would you like to start? This is, obviously, the first floor sitting room. Across the entranceway is a small library. All the books are gone I'm told. Some of those volumes would have been worth a lot, I think. They told me that the last owner sold all of them and most of the valuable antiques. This was after he realized that he was never going to recover the amount he had paid for this place. As I understand it, he then just disappeared, and the bank finally foreclosed. They've owned it for years. They've tried to have it torn down because the land would be worth quite a lot, but because of its age it's listed as an historic building and it can't be leveled. The bank would love to get rid of this thing so the current asking price is really a bargain." This elicited no reply.

Having wandered into the library as I spoke, my client, his voice slightly muffled by the dust mask, finally replied. "I believe there once was a fireplace in this room. You can see the chimney outside." This came as a surprise to me and I wondered how much he already knew about this house, and how he had discovered it. I tried to make light of the situation because I was already starting to feel somewhat uncomfortable about the client and the house. And there seemed to be a slight ringing in my ears.

"Oh, you've done some research. I found some notes at the office that said the fireplace is hidden behind that empty bookcase at the end of the room. There is supposed to be some secret lever that opens it up, but the notes didn't say where it was. This is clearly an interesting old house."

Illuminating the dark room with his lantern, the client moved around with almost a sense of ownership, as if he had been here before. As he passed the empty bookcase, I noticed that his hand lingered in the air for a moment and then he passed it by. Did he know the location of the lever? As he returned to where I was standing, he said, "Of course this isn't the real library. Do you know anything about the additional rooms below us?" This unsettled my nerves even further. Who was this person, and did he already have a connection to this ancient building? I replied as best I could.

"The basement? I don't know anything about the basement, or about any rooms down there. I guess there must be a furnace somewhere. This is my first time in this house and my notes don't say anything about the basement."

The client again ignored my words and headed slowly towards the back of the house. When he turned back to me he spoke quite firmly. "I think we need to take a look." He moved as if he knew where he was going. Making my way carefully through the darkness, avoiding the covered furniture, I followed the path of the client's lantern. I remember that this was where I started to feel slightly lightheaded and I actually shook my head a few times in an attempt to overcome my uneasiness.

Towards the back of the house there was a very old kitchen. The room was partially lit by the light entering a large window over the double sink, and that, combined with the client's light, enabled him to find a heavy wooden door. It was secured with a large hasp and padlock. Handwritten lettering warned "DO NOT ENTER – PRIVATE." I was now feeling very unsure of myself. I shook the lock, which held firmly, and I said, apologetically, "I'm sorry, I don't know anything about this, and I don't have a key to unlock it. I can call the office and see if they know anything."

The client had set down his lantern, seized the lock and, to my surprise, gave it an odd twist and a downwards yank and pulled it open. "I was once a locksmith. This type of lock is a piece of junk. Shall we?" And not waiting for a reply from me, the client, again seeming to know where he was going and using the light of his lantern for only basic guidance, slowly descended the heavy wooden steps. By now I was seriously considering ending this house tour and leaving this strange old building. However, lured, I suppose, by the possibility of a rather large commission should this old man actually buy the property, I followed more slowly as the light disappeared below me. Before I had reached the bottom I was again surprised, this time by the sudden appearance of light. I covered the last few steps more rapidly, turned to my right, and found the client, who had removed his dust mask, standing next to an electric panel. With an odd smile on his face he explained. "I noticed the breaker was not set; I reset it, and we have light. Please, have a seat."

I was now much too unnerved to sit down so, rather than complying, I started walking, slowly, around what appeared to be a large, and I noticed dust free, library. This one was filled with oversized, leather bound, apparently ancient texts. The few titles I could make out on the wide spines were in a strange alphabet, perhaps Asian or Arabic, which I could not read. What appeared to be a wide planked wood floor was covered, in places, with very old and well-worn Oriental rugs. I wondered if this meant there were more rooms below this one. There were several leather covered armchairs with floor lamps arranged beside them. As I continued around the room, I noticed my feeling of dizziness had increased and then realized that my whole body was starting to feel tired. I thought, and actually hoped, that perhaps I had finally contracted the flu. On some of the shelves around the room I noticed strange, almost grotesque carvings. Hanging high on the walls were pictures of which I could make no rational sense. They seemed to represent weird buildings covered in strange vegetation. And then I came upon a large tapestry hanging at one end of the long room and completely covering the wall. It depicted some sort of large multi-headed beast which was almost hidden in a yellow fog. As I watched, the tapestry seemed to move slightly, almost as if it was covering an opening in the wall through which a slight breeze was occasionally blowing. As I stood there, feeling almost hypnotically spellbound, the tapestry seemed to pulse; first moving slightly into the room, then pulling slightly away. All I could think of was a large animal slowly breathing. I returned to where the client had seated himself and, by now, feeling even my legs weaken, slowly eased myself into the chair next to him. I then realized with an unpleasant feeling, almost of dread, that the chair faced the tapestry at the end of the room.

Looking across at me, the client spoke slowly. "You are surprised at this collection of unusual artifacts. They are not like anything you're likely to see in a normal museum, I assure you. It was important that you'd never been down here. I asked your employer to send one of his newer agents. I said I enjoyed their enthusiasm." The client leaned back in his chair and clasped his hands together. He smiled enigmatically at me. By now both my body and my mind were completely unsettled, and his smile only added to my discomfort. He continued speaking.

"Now I'm going to tell you a little story," he began, "and at the end of it I'm going to ask you for a small favor. Oh, and while you're listening, please join me in a little of this old brandy which I brought along. It's quite nice." The client retrieved a silver flask and two small glasses from the pockets of his coat. He poured a bit in each glass and drank his own in one long swallow. Refilling his glass, passing the other to me, the client sat back in his seat and began the story. I could barely hold the small glass and dared attempt only a small sip. I felt no burn and tasted nothing.

"This shouldn't take long. But we have plenty of time. Sunset isn't for several hours. Howard Phillips Lovecraft, whom I hope you have heard of, lived not far from here in the early twentieth century. Both his parents were confined to and died in Butler Psychiatric Hospital, which is also located not far from here. Howard himself spent time in the same hospital.

"Howard was a writer of stories, and he wrote at least one story about this very house. He married a New York woman but found he could not live or find work in New York. When her business failed, they planned to move to Providence, but Howard's mother and two aunts would have nothing to do with this New York woman. Howard stayed in Providence and his wife moved to the Midwest. Well that's the official story. In the years that followed, Howard was able to write many stories, poems, and especially, letters, but he never achieved any real fame until after his death. He wrote mainly of the horror of the ancient ones, monsters and fiends which were held at bay only by strange forms of human sacrifice. Unfortunately, by the time Howard died he was absolutely stark raving mad. The official story was that he died from untreated intestinal cancer. Howard Phillips Lovecraft died of horror. People talk about having strange feelings 'in their gut.' Howard had gone way beyond a strange feeling. He had seen the horror and it had entered him. Finally, it killed him. The story about how his mother and aunts had driven his wife away? That was made up, probably by Howard. The truth was that he had tried to tell her about the horror. He had even brought her to this very room. Whether she herself saw the horror or just decided Howard was nuts, she was supposedly on the next train out of Providence. Or so the story goes." By now the client was leaning forward in his chair and his face was directly in front of mine. I realized that, although I desperately desired to, I was unable to pull back.

"It's important that you understand that the horror Howard wrote about was real, is real. And, indeed, a special kind of regular human sacrifice is required. The last one occurred when the Arkham Historical Society toured this property." And here the client sat back in his chair, his hands again clasped in front of him.

"Which brings us to today, and the little favor I'm asking of you. You may have noticed that your joints had started to feel a little funny and by now I expect you are completely unable to move. Oh, it wasn't the brandy; it was in the dust upstairs. The brandy was really for me, to celebrate this occasion. The first breath you took inside the house was all that was required. Then, when you shook out the drapes you really gave yourself a dose." The client paused, as if to allow me to understand what was happening. He resumed. "I'm sure you noticed the large tapestry at the end of the room. You can see it from where you are sitting. You may have seen it slightly move. And by now you may have deduced that behind it is an opening, an opening to the horror. So, the favor is simply, please, remain right where you are. Of course, you don't really have a choice." The client paused for a few seconds as, now unable to move at all, I attempted in vain to speak and then to scream. Then, with almost a smile on his face, the client continued. "Well, having told you my story and explained my request, it's now time for me to leave you. And, I'm afraid I'll have to leave you in the dark."

The client rose, picked up the small glass which had long since fallen from my hands, replaced his dust mask, and turned his lantern back on. He went to the electrical panel, selected a circuit breaker and turned out the lights. Now in the dark and unable to even turn my head, I listened to the footsteps going up the stairs and then the sound of the door closing, the hasp being swung into place and the lock being secured. I sat in the darkness, waiting.

Apparently all that I have just recounted happened over a year ago. I have been a patient at Butler Psychiatric Hospital and, I am told, been in a state of what the doctors call Acute Psychotic Trauma. I have exhibited an exaggerated fear of darkness, distant voices, and the smell of dust or mold. It has only been in the last several weeks, following a series of shock treatments that I have again become coherent and able to communicate rationally with the nurses and doctors. They tell me that I was discovered outside an old house on Benefit Street, huddled in a ball and crying. From documents in my pockets it was determined that I worked for a real estate company in Bristol, Rhode Island. When contacted, my employers said they had no idea what I was doing in Providence. They had not heard from me for two days and that my last house showing was supposed to have been in Barrington, but I had never arrived at the designated property.

And I am left wondering. How did this happen and why to me? Has "the horror" in fact entered me and is now waiting to manifest itself in some horrific way at some future unexpected time? Or, will I become a "client" and lead another agent into that house which still remains uninhabited on Benefit Street?

DARKNESS

I have to write this while there is still some light, before it becomes dark forever. Who could ever read this? I don't know but I have to write it. Have others also written? Are they writing now? I don't know.

Everything has gone wrong, just as it had to. Now, it appears so obvious, even to me. I am, or more accurately, was a librarian. I had a library of actual books. They were becoming rare and I maintained my collection as well as I could. I was never an engineer or a scientist and I didn't read those books. Now that it has happened it seems, even to me, to have been inevitable. I just wonder when it became inevitable to those people.

As long as I can remember, people talked about what was called climate change. At first, I understood that to mean only that winters would be colder—or warmer, and that confused me—and summers would be warmer. There were words like "greenhouse gases" and "carbon emissions." There was a discussion that things would be very bad if the temperature went up more than two degrees. That didn't make any sense to me either. Our winters were more than eighty degrees colder than our summers. The ice at both poles was melting faster than anyone had expected and the oceans were getting warmer and steadily rising. But the temperature changes were only a couple of degrees and the water was rising only a few inches. Most of us didn't see what the problem was.

There was increasing talk of sustainable non carbon emitting energy sources. I started to see big fields of solar panels outside the city and more panels on private homes. There were pictures of gigantic wind turbines out in the ocean. I never thought to ask where all these devices were made.

Then, one year, after much international discussion and threatening, the world agreed to stop burning coal. That decision caused major economic disruptions. There was rioting in the streets in places that had depended on coal for energy and jobs. At the same time droughts caused by changes in weather patterns were resulting in massive crop failures around the world. Famine and local wars and migrations followed. Nations with water and food were urged to reach out to the starving. In some cases they did, while they still could.

The average temperature rise was announced to have exceeded three degrees and at the same time the Replacement Scandal occurred. A report intended to have been kept secret was leaked to the public. There were charts and math and many words but the simple message was, "We cannot sustain and replace our solar panels and wind turbines without the intense power available from fossil fuels." Turning iron into steel, refining aluminum from bauxite and building solar panels required much more energy than renewable sources could provide. We could keep the lights and computers running, but not replace broken panels and wind turbines. At about the same time that the report was leaked, a major wind farm off Scotland was destroyed by massive waves and Oklahoma's major solar installation was severely damaged by a string of large tornados. Our government denied that panels and turbines could not be replaced and said we would continue to use a very low level of oil and natural gas for that purpose alone. They noted that the world's nuclear plants were all running smoothly and had decades of life remaining. All these statements turned out to be deliberate lies, to avoid panic it was later explained. There was already an international agreement to cease any and all use of any carbon based energy with the lone exception of wood for heating and cooking. The agreement could be enforced by airstrikes if necessary.

The nuclear power plants, which were all located near sources of what had been cold cooling water, were now shutting down automatically as the cooling water temperature had risen above the maximum allowed. Fortunately, the plants had been designed in such a way that these high temperature shutdowns could not be overridden. I never heard of any attempts to override, but by then there was no Evening News and the lights had gone out for most of the world.

People who were able had hoarded food and water and alcohol. They seemed to think that once all the carbon emission stopped, things would quickly get back to normal. That was a sadly mistaken dream. Even I could see that things were not going to even improve within the lifetime of anyone now alive.

There are, I believe, not that many people still alive. In addition to famine and wars there have been waves of disease caused by lack of sanitation and uncontrolled travel. As the final pockets of electric power disappeared, so also did the ability to pump water. And, of course, as the now consistent cloud cover intensified, solar panels became useless. And then, in the major cities of what was once called The First World, the strange phenomenon of Suicide Parties began. I will not attempt to describe them.

I have been very lucky. My small apartment is in the same building as many much larger ones, owned by people who hoarded food and water. They took their alcohol to the suicide party. I have been surviving on what they left behind.

I am outside, on the roof of the building, as I write this in near darkness. This, at approximately noon I think, is as bright as it ever gets in what I think is summer. Each day the clouds get thicker and it gets darker. Here we are, following the dinosaurs into extinction.

ALASKA 2018

An oddly large woman, on whose round ivory skinned face appeared a tiny crimson mouth, came down the aisle. Her straw-colored hair was pulled back tightly into what seemed to be a closely truncated ponytail. In a voice more suited to Minnie Mouse she inquired, row by row, "Would you like something to drink?"

Air Canada Flight 532 Vancouver to Boston was the final leg of a two week trip to Alaska. The most compelling result of two weeks in Alaska is an intense desire to return. Tundra to rainforest, oceans, glaciers, fiords, snow covered mountains; all these, plus a cruise ship crammed into two weeks.

Alaska, the Aleut word has been written as Alaxsxaq or Alyeska in an attempt to capture the very guttural native language. The sounds literally mean "The object toward which the action of the sea is directed." We might call that "the shore."

Regardless of the pronunciation, Alaska is immense. You could put the state of Rhode Island into Alaska 130 times. But, while the population of Rhode Island is slightly over one million, the population of Alaska is less than 750,000. Driving distance from Seattle to Anchorage, which is along the southern coast, is about the same as the driving distance from Gales Ferry,

Connecticut to Las Vegas.

Fairbanks, located in the middle of the state, is Alaska's third largest city with a population of 32,750. (The population of Norwich Connecticut is almost 40,000.) Today known as the "Golden Heart City," Fairbanks is the last stop of the Alaskan Railroad. It is the southern end of the Dalton Highway to the North Slope and the oil fields. The Alaskan pipeline runs just outside of town.

Fairbanks is classified as a desert; typical yearly precipitation is only about 12 inches, including the snow which is usually too cold to form into a snowball. A sign of spring is when you can actually form a snowball. Moisture laden clouds moving south from the Arctic Sea rise up to cross the mountains of the Brooks Range and drop their rain and snow. Likewise, rain and snow clouds coming north from the Gulf of Alaska drop their moisture as they rise to cross the Alaska range. Fairbanks lies approximately in the middle of the two mountain ranges.

Winter in Fairbanks is endured. Although in the summer the sun never really sets, in the winter the sun never really rises. Temperatures can reach 40 degrees below zero. (For you math nerds, 40 below is the same temperature in degrees Fahrenheit or Celsius.) At this temperature, even though your car has an oil warmer and an engine block warmer plugged in and operating, you will not try to start your car or truck because its fan belt will shatter into a hundred pieces.

Denali National Park lies a few hours by bus south of Fairbanks. At approximately 6 million wilderness acres the park is roughly twice the size of the state of Connecticut. Denali itself, for a while Mt. McKinley, rises 20,310 feet, making it the tallest mountain in North America. The park interior is accessible by one road which is open only during the three months of summer. The rest of the year the park is patrolled by rangers on dogsleds mushing from one lonely cabin to the next looking for distressed animals or hikers (they're out there) or the very rare poacher.

Denali and its neighboring peaks, Mt. Foraker (17,400 feet), Mt. Hunter (14,572 feet), and Mt. Hayes (13,832 feet) provide a range of snowcapped beauty which itself provides reason enough to come to Alaska. The animals, the glacial silt laden braided rivers, and the wildflowers are all eclipsed by the surrounding peaks.

Moose, bear, caribou, fox, wolves, Arctic hare, lynx, and ground squirrels survive in an ecological balance disturbed only occasionally by the human species. An experiment was once performed after an apparent crash in the Arctic hare population. The educated thought was that the wolf population had become too large. An area of the park was designated for wolf hunting and the remainder left to fend for itself — as it had done for the last 10,000 years or so. Of course, the area in which the wolves were hunted went way out of balance. The species the wolves would normally have controlled overpopulated, ran out of available food, and crashed. In the natural section things quickly returned to normal. The lesson learned seemed to be, "Sometimes bunnies do better than other times. Don't worry about it."

When moose calves are born in the spring, they have only about three months to gain the hundreds of pounds they will need to survive the long winter ahead of them. The favorite food of the moose is willow. This is not the large weeping willow, but more of a bush that can grow to a height of maybe eight feet. Wherever you see willow in the park you will, sooner or later, see moose. But even the willow has a survival scheme. Remember ecological balance? If it happens that there is an excessive moose population (maybe some idiot shot the wolves) and the willows are eaten almost down to the ground, they start to emit a poison. And things get back into balance.

Our guide, herself a onetime park ranger, dog musher, and mountain climber, told us a couple of Denali stories. One day while hiking in the back country she had settled down to watch a moose and her calf grazing along the edge of a river when our guide spotted a wolf sneaking towards them. Mama moose smelled the wolf and moved her calf under an overhang along the riverbank. The wolf, who for some reason had decided to try this alone, apparently had forgotten that wolves work best in packs. Our guide watched, hoping this would not get too ugly. The wolf attacked and was kicked forty feet into the air, landing with a resounding thud. He lay on the ground for a long time and when he arose, he did not look like a healthy wolf. Our guide doubted he would survive the coming winter. And this tale is a reminder of why the moose is the most dangerous animal in the park. Wolves and bears, unless they or their young are threatened, prefer to just walk away from people. Moose on the other hand will charge if a person gets within about twenty yards and will kick you forty feet into the air.

Another time our guide watched, from a safe distance, as a mama bear taught her two cubs to swim. Bears usually have twins. Literally a bear and a spare. The first cub took to the water immediately and was enjoying splashing around. The second cub was more of the "That's okay, I'll just watch," kind of a bear. Mama picked him up by the scruff and heaved him in. He stumbled out, shook himself off, and found himself again flying through the air into the cold water. It took a while but he finally got the idea and mama and cubs crossed the river and moved on. Both cubs now needed to fatten up before winter. Unlike the giant bears on Kodiak Island who subsist on a rich diet of salmon, the Denali grizzlies eat mostly berries and an occasional ground squirrel.

In what is referred to as the Upper Paleolithic Period, say

15,000 years ago, there was dry land where the Bering Sea now exists. Animals from North America went west and animals, and for the first time people, entered North America. Some of the people preferred to remain in what is now Alaska. Numerous tribes were established, and people, plants, and animals settled into an ecological balance. Tribes fought, some winters were worse than others, but life went on.

And then, in 1784 the white man, in the form of Russians, arrived, slaughtered hundreds of the Koniag people living where they landed, and began the mass slaughter of sea otters for their fur. After a bit the British arrived, and the Spanish and even the Italians, each setting up a little post and claiming it all for their king, queen, or patron. Eventually the Russians dominated, but by 1867 things were not going at all well in Russia and in order to raise some quick cash they sold what we now call Alaska to the United States, native people included at no extra cost.

When gold was discovered in the Klondike in 1896, tens of thousands headed north to stake their own claims in what now is part of Canada as well as parts of Alaska. Rail lines and roads were built through the mountains, snow, and ice. Some were more successful than others. Anchorage, Seward, and Fairbanks all became major settlements and the non-native population was established.

There are efforts now being made to recover, maintain, and grow what remains of the native cultures that still remain. Without a written language all traditions must be passed by word of mouth. Dances, songs, and rituals, none of them now relevant to modern life, other than as bits of history, are studied and performed by school children, encouraged more by grandparents than parents. And someday, it may all be gone as is the gold and as will be the oil and perhaps even the salmon.

A SEPTET FOR ROCKY

O kay, this is a difficult subject to talk about. I am pleased that so many of you were able to get here for this little ceremony. This beautiful overlook above Cape Disappointment where the Columbia River empties into the Pacific Ocean was of course one of his favorite spots. It is an awesome sight that over the decades has inspired terror in the hearts of many mariners. Inside the museum is a chart showing the hundreds of shipwrecks that have taken place within only a few miles of where we are now standing. Even today crossing the bar — the ever shifting sandbar that greets you as you attempt to move upstream — requires a specially trained bar pilot to guide each ship.

I am going to attempt to communicate how I felt about my friend. I knew him all his life. Did I love him? I don't think that word really applies to our relationship. He was always there when I needed him, and I hope I was there when he most needed me. We traveled together and, as I mentioned earlier, this location always seemed to make him happy. It was never, in spite of its name, a disappointment for him. As I look out over the rushing waters of the Columbia, I think of the flow of life up and down this river. Salmon, of course, as they swim up to spawn and then their offspring return to the Pacific to become part of the great family of creatures that inhabit these waters. Years later, they begin their own return up the river. Today we have already seen bald eagles soaring above us and black cormorants nesting below us. Although we won't see them, there are certainly bears and beaver in the woods along the river, both species feeding on the river's bounty and, when their time has come, becoming food themselves. And under the water, as the fresh river water blends with the salty sea, the variety of life is unimaginable. From the tiny krill to the immense whales and every size in between, the ocean is a constant reminder to us humans that we are not the only living beings on this planet.

I'm sure some of you were anticipating perhaps a scattering of ashes ceremony today. After all we are clearly not at a grave site. But there is no obvious urn of remains. I will keep you in suspense no longer. Earlier this week, one evening as the sun was setting, quite gloriously, into the ocean, I lowered Rocky's body into the river and watched him being swept away to become part of that beautiful complex ecosystem. His remains will be consumed, by which animals I'll never know. But I will know that the ones that consume Rocky will themselves be consumed by others and that my favorite dog will, in this way, really be able to endure forever.

CONNIE

The evening began with chilled imported champagne and a room-temperature brie. Connie refused to allow any of that cheap Italian "Pisseko" in her apartment and cheddar was for hamburgers. They sat together on her embroidery covered divan, each contemplating what pleasures might await them.

The large picture window of her Riverside Drive apartment presented a view of the Hudson River and a multi-hued sunset which was now defying any artist to fully capture it. They sat, not quite touching, not speaking, and watched the Earth slowly turn and force New Jersey to cover the last of the evening colors. As if taking her cue from the diminishing sunlight, Connie rose, turned on two small table lamps, and glided into her kitchen. When he started to follow, she firmly directed him to enjoy the lights of Riverside Park, finish the champagne and let her work.

At forty-two Connie had been engaged twice but had never married. As the wedding dates had approached, she had realized that she did not want to spend the rest of her life with that person. She had abandoned thoughts of marriage and children to allow herself to focus instead on her successful career in investment banking and her love: the preparation and consumption of excellent food. She found friends to dine with and, on occasion, to sleep with. She had met William, a lawyer, totally by chance at a performance at Lincoln Center. They had been seated next to each other, talked at intermission, went for a drink following the show and agreed to stay in touch. They had dined at restaurants of Connie's choosing, but this was the first time William had been invited to her apartment.

She took the preparation of food — cooking was for cafeterias — as seriously as others took religion or sex. The hunger she sought to assuage was not related to nutrition. She labored joyfully over the subtle mixture of flavors and textures that one could achieve with appropriate ingredients, technique, and the knowledge of how to use them. This meal had been conceived and prepared with a purpose. Although, as always, it was a test for herself, and she would grade herself harshly, it was also a test for William. If he scored well, it could produce a change in their relationship.

She summoned him to her candle lit dining table and the meal commenced. She began it with an herb bisque, whose extremely subtle flavors forced one to heighten both senses of smell and taste to fully appreciate the desired effect. When they had finished and William had complemented her work, Connie cleared the dishes and returned with two large plates. Each plate contained a portion of filet mignon (thirty-five dollars a pound at Zabar) with her own Béarnaise Sauce, roasted asparagus tips, and wild rice mixed with fresh sliced mushrooms. A bit of the Béarnaise was dripped lightly on the asparagus, this being one of Connie's favorite effects — how different the sauce tasted when eaten with the meat compared to how it tasted on the vegetable. As she ate, she watched

145

William carefully, already grading his performance. The beautiful Bordeaux she had poured was almost a meal in itself and Connie had also provided large water glasses to allow them to clear their taste buds between the cacophony of flavors she had presented.

After having sampled everything on his plate and the wine, William put down his fork, bowed his head and proclaimed "You are unquestionably the supreme mistress of the culinary arts. This is beyond magic. It's pure wizardry. Now please pardon me while I gleefully consume every morsel."

But there was, of course, even more to come. She cleared the large plates and returned with the salad. A loose mélange of butter lettuce, thinly sliced ripe avocado with a scattering of pomegranate seeds was lightly dressed with a mix of lemon juice and olive oil. They relaxed for a few moments following the salad, but then Connie removed those plates and returned with the dessert. This consisted of a rich flourless chocolate cake, topped with fresh raspberries, a few drops of raspberry liquor, and a small dollop of freshly whipped cream, more for appearance than taste.

When the final plates had been emptied, they both sat back in their chairs and William said, "That was wonderful. Thank you so much." Connie's reply was, "I'm glad you liked it."

She cleared the dessert plates from the table and brought them to the sink where she began to rinse them. William came up behind her, put his arms gently around her waist and softly murmured, "Are you in the mood for a little more dessert?" Connie turned, removed his hands from her waist, smiled and stared into his brown eyes. "And is this what you have really been waiting for, anticipating all evening?" she inquired, and before he could respond she moved past him to retrieve a wine glass from the table. As she returned to the sink Connie added, "My pleasure tonight was planning and preparing this meal for you, and of course enjoying it with you. Apparently, the meal was not sufficient. It was not the pleasure you had been hoping for. I think you should run along now and maybe some time we'll grab a quick meal somewhere and you can take me back to your place and demonstrate how well you can cook."

THE NEXT IN LINE

I

In the center of the spacious room, not against any wall, was a large bed of the four-poster style. Headboard, footboard, and the tall corner columns were of dark well-polished mahogany. Along the eastern wall were three tall windows, arched at the top and now covered by light curtains which admitted most of the late morning sunshine. Pulled to the side of the two outer windows were heavy dark crimson drapes, available for blocking all light from both the outside and the inside.

There were no side tables accenting the bed, nor were there any chairs in the room. A large bureau was the only other piece of furniture. On the polished bureau top on a white lace mat lay a silver comb, brush, and mirror ensemble, each highly polished and reflecting the light from the large chandelier which hung in the exact center of the room almost over the foot of the bed.

The bed was covered with an oversized duvet which reached almost to the floor on each side. The duvet cover of scarlet silk seemed out of place in the otherwise formally staid bedroom. Equally unexpected were a half dozen pillows cased in a variety of scarlet and black, piled at the head of the bed.

A large rug of Oriental design, presenting figures of what may have been ancient Eastern deities, odd structures, and assorted exotic animals, covered most of the floor. The bed stood entirely on the rug.

Her grandmother had spent the final years of her life in this room and had died, at the age of ninety-eight, in that bed. In the years that had followed the house had been maintained by the resident staff, which by now had been reduced to two maids and an occasional handyman or groundskeeper. Her grandmother's substantial estate paid for the upkeep and took care of taxes and any other expenses associated with the house and grounds.

As she surveyed the room, Constance tried to imagine who had removed the rest of the furniture and then chosen the garish colors for the duvet covering and the pillows. She would ask one, or probably both of the two older women who had greeted her. She thought she recalled their names as Beth and Nell. Why, at their advanced ages, were they still introducing themselves as young girls? Why weren't they Mrs. This and Mrs. That? Had they really lived in this strange house since her grandmother had hired them maybe fifty years ago?

Constance had a strong urge to sit and contemplate the room and consider her own new situation, but as she had observed, there were no chairs. She did not find the bed at all inviting. She stood there, just inside the doorway and tried to find or feel something of her grandmother, but failing that, turned and walked toward the staircase.

The three women sat around the large circular oak table in the center of the kitchen. The room appeared spotless and Constance realized that there was no refrigerator, although a large stove and a dishwasher, both clean to the point of appearing brand new, were in place. There was an empty spot where a refrigerator could once have stood. She also noted the lack of any small appliances such as a mixer, a toaster, or even a coffee maker. Not remembering which woman had which name, Constance looked at a spot between the two and asked, "When was the last time anyone actually used this kitchen?

The two women, both with gray hair and tired expressions, looked at each other, then one replied. "Oh, that would have been the year she died. Your grandmother that is. I'm sorry; I know you just lost your mother." There was a pause. "And I saw you looking where the fridge used to be. We had it moved downstairs to our quarters. He said it was alright. Of course, if you want to move in, it can be moved back." Another pause followed as Constance tried to process what she had just heard. "Oh, and I'm Nell, she's Beth."

Constance tried a smile as she looked from the two women to the kitchen window and along the empty walls. Through the clear clean glass in the kitchen cabinet doors she could see only empty shelves. Had the dishes followed the refrigerator? Then, looking more towards the center of the table than at either woman, Constance spoke. "I've known this was coming for years. Even before my mother got sick, she and I talked about this place. My mother of course, you were here then, grew up in this house, but I don't think I remember ever spending even a single night here. We visited Grandmother a few times every year. I remember eating in the big dining room. But it seemed as if my mother couldn't get away from here fast enough. When my grandmother was near the end, I think my mother even stayed in the motel in town rather than stay here. She never told me why she was so averse to this building. When my father would, almost jokingly, say, 'Someday this will all be yours,' she would almost sadly respond, 'Please, don't remind me.' So, here I am, and I must confess I have no idea what to do." She stopped and then, looking at Nell asked, "Would it be possible to get a cup of coffee or tea or even just a glass of water? I'd get it myself, but I don't see any cups or glasses."

It was Beth who replied. "Why, of course, Ma'am. Which would you prefer? You said coffee first, so that's probably what you would prefer. I can run downstairs and fix it in a jiffy."

Nell turned to Beth and said with a smile, "And when was the last time you ran anywhere?" Turning to Constance she said, "If you wouldn't mind, Ma'am, we could all go down to our quarters and sit. It's not as bare or quite as neat, but it will be more comfortable. I've never liked these wooden chairs."

Constance smiled, this time warmly, stood up and said, "That sounds very nice. I've never been downstairs. And please, call me Connie. I'm not ready for Ma'am."

II

"Bitch!"

"Oh?"

"Not you Sheila."

"Well, that's nice. Who then?"

"All of them actually, but I was thinking of my sister."

"You mean Constance? Why doesn't anyone call her Connie?"

"Yes her. I only have one sister!"

"Oow, aren't you in a mood. What'd she do now?"

"She went up to the house without me."

"The house? What house?"

"Oh, I never mentioned the family manse in New England?"

"Really?"

"Oh, really. I guess she thinks she has to deal with it all by herself. Maybe she does. It has always been 'No boys allowed.'"

"What the hell are you talking about? Are you rich or something?"

"Ha! I wish. Our mother died and the terms of the estate leave everything to Constance as the oldest surviving daughter."

"So, she's a sweet sister and sells the old place and splits the money with you. That'd be nice. You could take me on a cruise."

"Why don't you get us both a beer and I'll tell you a story about our family's maybe haunted house."

"I don't want one and you don't need one. So, start talking."

"Okay, we'll do this stone cold sober. Maybe it'll make more sense that way.

"Some time around the turn of the last century, say 1905, my great grandfather made a lot of money. No one has ever told me how. Maybe nobody knows. So, he was this big deal business guy in New York, and he had acquired this sweet little wife. In order to spend more time alone in the city with his several lady friends, he built a big country house in New England and settled his wife in it. He piled on all the luxuries possible and provided servants to wait on her and take care of the house and the rather extensive grounds. At some point great granny got knocked up by her husband on one of his visits, or the gardener, I don't know. We don't talk about that. And thus appeared my grandmother. Soon after, great granny, becoming a little older and wiser, made her move. She found an apparently excellent lawyer and filed for divorce on all sorts of grounds. The lawyer demanded everything: the house, stocks, bonds, and whatever cash was available. He almost got it all. Great granddad was left with just enough to live happily and continue to enjoy his women friends."

"So great granny was sitting pretty. And she left it all to your grandmother?"

"Well, it's more interesting than that. Great Granny was a very smart woman, or at least she knew the right people. When the 1929 stock market crash came along, she was one of the very few people who actually made money. And some time after that she found another smart lawyer and set up the girls only inheritance scheme."

"The what? You can do that?"

"I guess you can 'cause she sure did. The way it works is that the entire estate goes to the oldest surviving daughter on the death of her mother. And that was my grandmother. Then when granny died nine years ago it all went to my mother. Now she's dead and it all goes to Constance."

"How nice for her. But she'll at least throw you a few bucks?"

"So I can take you on a cruise?"

"Well, that too."

"It's not at all that simple. There is, apparently, a curse that goes with the estate. Remember, Great Granny was still some pissed when she set this thing up. The first example of the curse was Great Granddad. Shortly after the divorce settlement was finalized, he was hit by a streetcar and died on the spot. Freak accident right? Except, one of his lady friends was with him at the time and she swore that he thought he saw his ex—Great Granny—on the other side of the street and was running to talk to her when he was flattened."

"Umm, and that makes a curse? Where was your Great

Granny at the time?"

"She was in the house, far away, hosting a tea party with the neighborhood ladies.

"That was not at all the only example of the curse. My grandfather was very angry when Granny inherited all that money and the house and had gone to his lawyer to see if they couldn't do something about it to let him control the money."

"And he was hit by a bus as he left?"

"Noooo, better than that. He was shot in the lawyer's office by a guy who was furious at the lawyer for helping his wife divorce him. He kicked the door open and started shooting. Missed the lawyer but killed Grandpa."

"Okay, you're just making this up to amuse me, right?"

"I wish I was."

"Okay, so when Granny died your mom inherited everything and, I don't want to ask, but…"

"Yeah, what became of my dad? You just realized that you have never met him, and I have never mentioned him. Well, he believed in the curse and decided the safest thing to do was to skedaddle. Of course, he took some girl along with him, and maybe that caused it."

"It?"

"They both died in a fiery wreck when his Subaru was t-boned by a gasoline truck."

"So, last year your mother died and now Constance is up there trying to decide what she should do. But she doesn't have a daughter. She doesn't even have a boyfriend! So, what happens?"

"That, Sheila, is what I had hoped to discuss with her before she went to the house. But now that she's there, everything is up to her. I clearly have no control. Can I have that beer now? Or

154

maybe I should wait on you."

III

From the outside the house just looked tired. Constance was sitting on the stone bench which had been placed on the lawn island in the center of the circular driveway. She could almost remember sitting here with her brother long ago. And, she realized, it was not a happy memory. But now she could not remember why just sitting here brought back that emotion. The four tall first floor windows, two on each side of the front door, were closed off from the sunlight by thick white drapes which ought to have been opened by now. She guessed that both Beth and Nell, those teenage names, saw no reason to make the effort since they were the house's only inhabitants. Constance remembered the large room on the right. It had been called the company room and she had never been allowed in it as a child. Even as an adult she could not remember being in it. The two windows on the left opened into the dining room with its long mahogany table and large dark wood sideboards along the walls. The kitchen lay on the backside of the house and connected, through a pantry, to the dining room. In back of the company room was the library. She wondered if any of the old books remained. Surely they would not have been discarded.

She sat, alone, trying to accept the enormity of the fact that this house, everything in it, the many surrounding acres and whatever money remained, now all belonged, totally, to her. No one else, even her brother Ray, could make any claim on it. Thinking of Ray, she recalled what he had always called "the curse." Up until high school, when their father had died, she had always laughed at the idea. It had seemed absurd. But then, in the midst of her first real teenage love, she had imagined what might lie ahead if the curse was true. Any man she became close to could be in danger. She wondered what if there was no marriage. What if there was never a daughter? It was all too scary. And that day she walked away from one confused boyfriend and had remained alone until now. She had actually wondered what would happen if she married a woman, although she had no feelings for other women. They could arrange for a pregnancy and provide a female heir. And then who would have to die? But she also wondered if the curse did not, in fact, exist. What if those men had died of strange accidents? Was she missing out on a full life with a loving husband and happy children running up and down the many stairs in that big old house? Children she would certainly allow into the company room. Was she wasting her happiness for something that had never existed? Constance sat on the hard bench and looked at the house. Clouds had covered the morning sun and a breeze had developed. It was probably going to rain.

TERRY

She was an exceptionally good-looking woman. I think now that "pretty" is a word for girls in their teens and not grown women. She was also certainly attractive. I had been immediately attracted. Of course, part of that attraction could have been her long wavy red hair, which was gathered in a soft ponytail that hung over her left shoulder. And maybe the rum.

I have at least two problems with rum. One is that I like the taste of it. Put a couple of shots of dark rum in a tall glass filled with ice cubes and then fill it with ginger beer or cola and you have a drink. I don't try to resist. A second problem is that rum sneaks up on me. Beer or wine gives me a quick buzz which slowly fades away. Rum does the opposite. At first, I feel nothing beyond the pleasant taste, maybe have another one. Time passes and I realize that I am now "under the influence."

So, there I sat, clearly "under the influence" looking across Sara's swimming pool at a red-headed woman I had never seen before. This was another of Sara's "mostly singles" pool parties. People started drifting in around five, some dressed for an afternoon party with shorts and tank tops and Hawaiian shirts. And some were dressed for an evening party. Summer dresses with lots of color for the women and slacks and shirts for the men. The redhead had on a dress of many colors that draped her shape quite nicely. I enjoyed watching her. She was talking to Sara and seemed to be pointedly ignoring the guy who was standing with them. She had turned her body towards the pool and effectively put him behind her right shoulder. She looked even better from the front than she had from the side. And then Sara looked across the pool directly at me. The redhead followed Sara's gaze and I was the focus of four female eyes.

At that point in my life I was between wives and not looking for the next one, even a redhead; especially not a redhead. I planned to reach the age of forty and still be single. After that I figured I could settle down and enjoy a boring middle age. It was a nice self-centered life with no commitments outside of work and a few monthly bills. I pursued short term relationships which lasted a few weeks before we aimlessly went our separate ways. And now Sara and the redhead were coming around the pool with that guy trailing behind them. I tried to sit up from my slouch.

Terry sat down next to me as Sara introduced us and then dragged away the man who had followed. Quite fog headed and desperate to begin a brilliant conversation I managed to blurt out, "So, who was that with Sara? I think I've seen him before." Terry looked after Sara and almost laughing replied, "That was Brad, who proudly informed me that it was short for Bradford who was some sort of whoop-de-do in the Civil War or maybe the Revolutionary War."

My inane response was, "Well, not to worry, I am proud to say I come from a long line of nobody in particulars." I paused, then, fearful of a lull in the conversation rambled on. "I wonder if there is a club I should join. Maybe there's a special tie or, yes, a secret handshake. That's what we need. Wait, are you famous for something?"

Now Terry was laughing. "Sara said you were funny, but she failed to point out you were half plotzed. But that's okay. You're the third person Sara has introduced me to tonight and the first one who seems at all interesting and has me laughing. Plus, I agree with Sara, you are cute."

Ignoring the compliments, I said, "Wait, I'm only third on Sara's list of eligible bachelors? I'm crushed."

Terry reached over and put her very warm hand on mine and said, "Don't be. Your friend Stan—he said he was your friend—nearly assaulted us as we came out the door and as soon as Sara got rid of him Bradford arrived, prepared, I'm sure, to invite me to the Generals' Ball. But, at last, here we are." This time there was a pause, but before I panicked and said something really stupid Terry took away her hand and stood up saying, "I hope you brought your bathing suit because I want us to jump into that pool. Shall I go change?"

I managed, "I did, you shall and so will I," hoping I could actually stand up, find my suit, get it on, and navigate back out here. The pool was an excellent idea. Maybe I could escape the "influence."I succeeded in getting into my bathing suit and returning to the pool and was sitting on the edge when Terry emerged from the house wearing a smooth fitting electric blue one-piece bathing suit. She performed a pirouette and asked, "You like?"

"What's not to like?" I replied.

"That's funny, you don't look Jewish!" she yelled as she plunged into the water.

I followed immediately and felt the slow emergence of sobriety as the cool water covered my body. Terry had moved to the deep end and of course I pursued her. As I got close enough, she wrapped both arms around my neck and started a serious merger of our mouths. I put my arms around her, and we slowly sank towards the bottom of the pool. I remember thinking, "So this is how I drown, passionately kissing a partially naked, exceptionally good-looking redhead at the bottom of a swimming pool. Again, what's not to like?" As our feet hit bottom, we both let our knees bend and then straightened out our legs and kicked up to the surface, where we broke the kiss and for the first time actually looked into each other's eyes. I ventured, "Well that was nice." Terry responded, "Now that I have your attention, let's do some laps. The pool is almost deserted." And she started stroking towards the shallow end. Terry was a good swimmer and I had a hard time catching her, and then keeping up with her after she turned and started back. We did five or six laps and then Terry stopped and pulled herself out to sit on the edge. We were at the midpoint of the pool and I remained standing in the water. She looked down at me and asked, "Are we having fun yet?"

"I've been having fun ever since you sat down next to me," was my reply.

"Good," she said. "Now come up here next to me and let's plan the rest of the night."

Our affair lasted almost a year, during which I met her children – she had two – her parents, and her sister. We all got along on a friendly basis, but I felt we were never actually that close. Terry and I went to Bermuda together and even tried skiing that winter, but by spring it seemed as if we were both bored. Were we bored with each other or our situation? Aside from being occasionally fun, it just felt pointless. It was not until a couple of years later, when I heard she had remarried, that I realized there had never been any real love between us. We certainly enjoyed each other's company. We liked each other, hell we lusted for each other. But, in the end, we never loved each other.

SUZANNE

I

The sun had not yet cleared the taller of the dew laden trees. Across the paved path, a fairway rolled out towards a distant putting green, the grass still wet from an early morning sprinkling. The soft stillness was broken only by the repetitive "pock, bounce, pock, bounce," sounds of a tennis ball being volleyed by two women. Each of them was wearing matching colors; the older wore a green and white Sarah Lawrence sweatshirt and green shorts, the younger wore a powder blue skirt and a snug fitting powder blue shirt. Both wore white tennis shoes. The younger of the two also sported a white billed visor cap and her long blond ponytail hung from the back of it. Occasionally there was the odd sound of the ball hitting the net, followed by a few indistinguishable words before the volleying restarted. The court on which they were playing was still shaded from the heat of the morning sun and they continued to enjoy the quiet coolness of the early hour.

A white Mercedes convertible was parked in the small lot adjacent to the tennis court, and in it sat a young man attentively watching the younger of the two women. Her ponytail swayed as she smoothly glided across the court and her blue skirt softly draped first one hip, then the other. She was slim and clearly athletic, her skilled movements an affirmation of earlier hours spent on other tennis courts. He had not seen her since the last day of eighth grade. She was the daughter of wealth and he was the son of a car salesman and their worlds had only seldom intersected. The year following eighth grade she had been sent to a boarding school followed by college, and then time spent somewhere in Europe with her father. Watching her now he could almost sense the layers of refinement and education that had been applied to that once skinny little girl. And even though he was now the owner of a luxury car dealership and through it a full-fledged member of the country club, he still felt himself to be an outsider. The other club members were certainly friendly and never in any way condescending, but he could never get over a subtle feeling that he just did not belong here. Sitting in this $90,000 roadster, he was really just a delivery boy. Her mother had purchased the car as a gift for her daughter and he was just delivering it. And yet, he felt, maybe now that he had, in some sense, moved up in the world, there was a chance that he and the girl could be friends if not completely as equals. He hoped he was no longer the shy little boy she had once known. He sat, watching her play and hoping.

As the sun finally cleared the treetops and spread onto their playing surface, the older of the women called out something and started to walk off the court. Her daughter followed, but not before purposefully hitting the yellow ball up and over the surrounding fence and into the woods.

"Suzanne, why must you always do that? We do pay for those balls and they are reusable, you know."

"I just like to end a game with a little flourish and the cost of a tennis ball, I mean, really?"

The mother then pointed toward the parking area and said something to her daughter.

The girl noticed, first the convertible and then the boy sitting in it. She stopped walking and almost laughing exclaimed, "Oh my God! Is that Teddy?" She looked at her mother for confirmation and, having received a nod and a smile, gracefully strode towards the Mercedes. When she reached it, she slowly circled the car, finally returning to the passenger door, which she opened, and smoothly lowered herself into the plush leather seat.

"This is quite elegant, and you're looking pretty good yourself. I suppose my mother arranged this encounter, but when did you get this car?"

Ted hesitated, trying to form a coherent sentence, and managed to utter, "Suzie, you are looking fantastic. I would not have recognized you. It's been a long time." And after a short pause, during which the two just looked at each other, he added, "The car is from my dealership."

"It's beautiful! And I'll call you Ted if you will please call me Suzanne. I left Suzie the day they sent me off to Miss Pruitt's. So, this is your car?"

"No, actually, it's yours." And with these words he went from a temporary feeling of equality with Suzanne and all the club members, back into his role as just another delivery boy. He opened the door and stepped out of the car. Suzanne, still in a mild state of disbelief, opened her door and walked around to the driver's side. Feeling now as if he were a valet parking attendant, he handed her the keys and stepped away. She stepped in and snuggled herself comfortably into the driver's seat.

Now, apparently oblivious to his existence, she spoke to no one in particular "Oh, thank you Mommy. I did not expect anything like this."

She then sat quietly inspecting the car's interior, put her hands on the steering wheel and then dropped her right hand smoothly onto the shift lever. She bounced a little in the leather seat and issued a breathy "Yes!" She sat, quietly for a few moments, almost visibly taking ownership and becoming one with her new toy. Then, as if suddenly remembering he was there, but without actually looking at him, she gave the keys back to Ted saying only, "Oh, can you hold these? I need to go change." She opened the car door, swung her long tanned legs out, stood up and, without a further word, trotted back towards the club house. He watched her go and with her departure she took any thoughts he might have had of even a platonic friendship. She had, in a brief moment, confirmed his feelings of inadequacy. To these people he would always be that car salesman's son. To Suzanne, he was already nearly invisible.

II

It was almost half an hour after she had departed that Suzanne returned from the direction of the club house. She wore a creation of silk-like material in small flowery patterns of various shades of blue. It clung softly to one long leg then the other as she strode towards the car. Her tennis shoes had been replaced with delicate blue sandals and her hair, no longer in a ponytail, swept down her back over the softly tanned skin exposed by the low-cut back of the dress. She carried a small gold purse and wore oversized designer sunglasses.

Ted, although he still held the keys, felt he had no further right to sit in what was now Suzanne's car and had found a small bench on which to await her return. Both the bench and the car remained shaded by the tall graceful elms surrounding the tennis court. Alone, he had again allowed himself to feel part of this crowd, but as soon as Suzanne came into view those thoughts dissolved. She moved like a movie star. She looked like a fashion model. She was a beautiful princess from a land to which he would never be admitted. He stood and, preparing to surrender the keys and phone for a ride back to work, started slowly towards the car.

"Ted, what are you doing over there? Get in. We have to take this beauty for a ride. How much time can you spend with me today?"

Very surprised by the question, Ted hesitated then replied, "As long as you like. I'm the boss now." He quickly ran to the passenger side, got in, and passed her the keys. She paused, turned to him, the keys still in her hand, and spoke through a warm smile.

"Before we do anything, I owe you an apology for just handing you the keys and running off, as if you were some parking attendant. I was still a little overwhelmed by this car, but that's no excuse. While I have been doing nothing much more than smiling and looking pretty you have built your dad's car lot into a major luxury car empire. I should be holding the keys for you. Can we just start all over, Ted and Suzanne, reunited friends?" Overwhelmed himself, Ted managed to reply, "I'd like that."

"Well alright! We are off to Lighthouse Point along that nice winding Ocean Drive." And as if she had been driving the car for months, Suzanne started it, put it in gear and accelerated out of the parking area and onto the road. They passed in front of the club's main building and between beautifully groomed fairways, stopping once to allow two golf carts carrying a color-fully dressed morning foursome to cross. After a few turns they had reached the beginning of the coast road and Suzanne enjoyed the car's ability to rapidly accelerate. Ted had often taken clients for test drives along this route, but he had never experienced it at this speed. Suzanne, blond hair buffeting her shoulders, drove with precision, smoothly entering and exiting turns, taking full advantage of the car's capabilities. To their left stood the waterfront estates that had been there for many years and to the right the blue Atlantic, today adding white caps to the sun induced sparkle of the water. Just offshore a large sloop under full sail completed the picture of nautical beauty. Ignoring mansions, sea, and sailboat, Ted's eyes remained on Suzanne, still marveling at her change of attitude towards him. Her physical beauty as well as her skill and obvious enjoyment driving her new car, combined with her offer of friendship as equals, filled him with a warm sense of excitement and pleasure.

They arrived at the small deserted parking lot adjacent to the lighthouse. Suzanne stopped the car, turned off the engine, and much to his astonishment threw her arms around Ted's neck and gave him a warm kiss, exclaiming, "That was so fun!" Before he could react at all she had retracted her arms, opened her door and stepped out, calling back to him, "Come on let's walk on the beach." She pulled off her sandals and he removed loafers and socks and they set out down the deserted beach. As if recalling the Suzie of her youth, Suzanne ran in and out of the water's edge, holding the hem of her dress just above the run-up of broken waves. Ted remained on the wet sand just above the water and watched this cultured woman of wealth enjoy the simple pleasures of childhood. He didn't know whether he was about to laugh or cry from happiness when she came to him, took his hand, and shouted, "Let's run!" And, together, they dashed down the beach, by now both laughing with childish glee. When they finally stopped Suzanne dropped his hand and, putting both hands on her knees, took deep breaths. Then she turned back towards the car, walking slowly now and occasionally picking up a seashell which, after a close examination, she threw into the waves. She was now quiet and may have been thinking deep thoughts or nothing at all. Ted, watching her as she moved along, wished he knew. Was it at all possible that she was thinking about him?

When they were back in the car Suzanne, looking genuinely disappointed, said, "I wish we could continue this all day, but I have to have "luncheon" with mother and the ladies, and after this car I really can't skip it. You probably have to do something to keep your cars flying out the door too. Oh, I just remembered what I wanted to ask you. Do you play tennis?"

Ted mentally thanked his father for demanding that he take tennis lessons and learn how to play well as part of their joining the Country Club. He replied enthusiastically, "I do!"

"Great. I'll see if I can get that early morning spot. I assume that, being the big boss, you can skip work two mornings in a row? Oh, and I will warn you right now, I'm not that great but if I think you are trying to let me win, I will jump over the net and beat you senseless with your own racket. Got it?" He smiled and nodded agreement, feeling more and more that he was ready to skip work and join her any instant Suzanne might allow him to.

The ride back to the dealership was slower than the drive to the beach. Was Suzanne trying to stretch out their time together or was she just being sensible? She still seemed to enjoy every curve of the road and the precision handling of the

Mercedes. Neither of them spoke. Ted was already thinking about tomorrow and what might follow a game of tennis. Was the princess going to allow him into her royal realm after all?

III

Suzanne's Summer

This surely has been a summer of surprises for me. It has been almost magical. But my entire life has been one wonderful surprise after another, and I feel as if I should ask "why am I so lucky?" But that, as my father would say, is a meaningless question. Was it luck to be born into this family in this place in this time? I could not have been born to any other family in any other place at any other time. It wouldn't have been me. But, really, what a summer.

My mother and her friends met me at the airport with flowers, hugs, kisses, and a white stretch limo to take us home. It seemed to be all perfume, hugs, and kisses. A few days later she suggested we play tennis at the club and when we finished, she presented me with a beautiful Mercedes roadster, "Something to drive this summer." I was temporarily speechless. And who should be sitting in the driver's seat but my childhood friend Teddy Peasely who, it turns out, runs a luxury car business. He was no longer a shy little boy with glasses. He had actually become handsome! We started off a little awkwardly, though. I called him Teddy and he called me Suzie, but we got our 'grown-up' names straightened out and then, like a jerk, I just handed him the keys and ran off to change out of my tennis clothes. I'm terrible. I'm just so used to being waited on that I treated poor Teddy, I mean Ted, as if he was the parking valet. I was in such a hurry to drive that car I just forgot there was a world outside my own little bubble.

It was no surprise that the car drove beautifully. I went along the water out to the lighthouse, probably a little too fast for Ted's comfort but it felt wonderful. I think I gave him a big kiss when we stopped. I was so happy. I hadn't been to that spot for years and I just ran down the beach as if I was still a little girl. The cold water and wet sand on my bare feet made me feel wonderful. I often forget that the simplest things that don't even have a price tag can be so life affirming and just plain fun. It occurred to me that during the last years of European high society I never had much fun. I had many meaningful, empowering experiences, but not much big smile fun.

Ted and I played tennis the next morning before the sun got too high and it was almost embarrassing. I had just thrown on some old shorts and a sweatshirt. Ted had dressed as if he was going to play on center court at Wimbledon. And I had told him not to dare go easy on me, but it turned out that I had to let him win a few points. He played as if he had just learned and hadn't really played all that much. But I have to admit, it was more fun than just volleying with my mother. It was better than that. It was fun. And he was so nice trying to explain that he wasn't really trying to lose, that I was 'very good.' And later that week we played miniature golf and then went to Dairy Queen — almost as if we were teenagers on a date. Teddy, Ted, can be so sweet. He seems as if he is still a little boy in many ways. I guess that's why I still think of him as Teddy, rather than Ted. The rest of the summer Teddy and I spent a surprising amount of time together just doing silly fun things. He found a zip-line park and we spent half a day climbing on rope ladders and zipping through the trees. Who would ever have expected to see me doing things such as that? And it was all such fun. One day we took my new car and drove north along the coast to eat fried clams and lobster rolls! One surprise after another.

Of course, the biggest surprise of the summer was yet to come. My father was coming home for a while and he was bringing what he referred to as "an unexpected surprise." I remember thinking, "Aren't all surprises unexpected? Isn't that what a surprise is?" And, as he always seems to be, Daddy was correct. That surprise was unexpected.

Ted's Summer

It was a very surprising summer. I think it started on that first day when Suzanne kissed me. Even now I can still feel her lips on mine and the smell of her hair. I can see her in that beautiful clinging blue dress, running down the beach in and out of the water. I can still hear her laughter and feel the warmth of her hand in mine. That was our only kiss of the summer, but it meant so much to me. I took it as a badge of acceptance. Suzanne was all I could think of for the next two months. I could close my eyes and see her face. Part of me expected her to just stop answering my calls, but that didn't happen. So, I kept calling. I tried to think of things we could do together. I asked people at work for suggestions. And I managed to come up with things that Suzanne seemed to like. Although, to my surprise, she often told me, "I've never done this before!" And that little remark should have reminded me how far apart our worlds really were.

I often found myself wondering where this relationship

could go. It often felt as if we were brother and sister. We were close, but not in a romantic way. I hoped that would change. I didn't dare do or even say anything that might wreck what we had. So, things stayed the same, until the Big Surprise.

Suzanne's father spent much of each year in Belgium doing international business. I never did understand Suzanne's explanation of what that was. Clearly it involved making money, lots of money. Suzanne called me one morning, all excited, and said her father was coming home in a week and there would be a big reception for him at the club. She told me to wear my best suit because she wanted me to meet her father. She added that he had promised to bring her a big surprise. She said she wanted me there to catch her if she swooned. I hadn't bought a new suit in years, but I knew a great place to get one. And if there was to be any swooning and catching in front of her parents, I wanted to be the one doing the catching.

Well it was a big surprise. I had arrived a little early and Suzanne was not yet there. The club's Reception Room was nicely decorated. Although the summer was ending, there was not a sign of a pumpkin or the traditional colors of orange and black. Instead, each of the tables had a small vase with fresh flowers in fall colors. There were no hanging decorations at all. About a dozen people, older couples, friends of Suzanne's parents I assumed, were holding glasses and making small talk. I finally found her mother, who gave me a very odd look. It made me feel that she had not expected me. She kept looking at me and it was as if I could see the wheels turning in her head. After a moment she must have resolved her apparent problem. She broke into a big smile and said I should meet Suzanne's father. He was clearly the tall man across the room talking to several people. She led me to him. He was all smiles and greeted me with "Hello Teddy — oh I'm sorry, my daughter tells me I'm to call you Ted now. I must say you are quite different from the last time I saw you. Much improved, I'd say. And very successful I hear. Good for you." There was a slight pause, each of us wondering what to say next and then, looking around the room, he continued. "Oh, certainly you'll want to meet Andrew. He's, of course, the big surprise. He finished up his dissertation four months early, so I brought him home with me."

And I hoped, really hoped, that Andrew was a brother that Suzanne had failed to mention all summer. The next sentence ended that hope and many others.

"I'm sure she has told you that they are getting married next spring."

I was stunned. And, as my head stopped spinning, I realized that I didn't want to be there when Suzanne arrived. If she even noticed me once she saw Andrew, it would be embarrassing and confusing for both of us. Even then I didn't want to cause Suzanne the slightest bit of anxiety. I pulled my cell phone from my pocket, pretended to read a text, and made up some story about an emergency somewhere. As I was leaving, I noticed Suzanne's mother watching me. Her face had a sympathetically sad expression. And she mouthed the words, "Thank you." I had resolved her problem in the way she had hoped I would.

IV

A pair of light blue women's running shoes with white athletic socks stuffed into them lay on the seawall in the bright morning sun. Aside from the steady repetitive sounds of the arrival and retreat of the small waves and the occasional scream of a soaring gull, the beach was quiet. Slowly the calm was interrupted by the sounds of an approaching automobile. An expensive white convertible purred into a parking spot, the engine stopped, and the calm returned.

A young man wearing tan trousers, a brown tweed driving cap, and a dark brown jacket left the car and appeared pleased to discover the blue shoes on the seawall. He removed his loafers and socks, neatly rolled up the cuffs of his pants, and walked onto the beach. Shading his eyes against the bright sun, he looked in each direction along the sand until, way off to his right, he spotted what he was looking for.

Suzanne was walking slowly towards her shoes. She was moving along the edge of the water, sometimes running away from a particularly large wave. Her eyes were looking down, searching for interesting shells. When she found one to her liking she stopped, picked it up, studied it briefly and then, turning towards the sea, threw it as far as she could. It was after one of these tosses, while she was resuming her search, that she saw Andrew in the distance waving his arms to attract her attention. Not yet ready to leave her waves and shells, Suzanne pretended not to see him and continued her leisurely search.

Finally, when she could no longer honestly ignore his shouts, Suzanne looked up, as if seeing him for the first time, and gently waved in return. She did not, however, hasten her pace and continued slowly examining the water's edge. Andrew would have to wait.

But Andrew had chosen not to wait and was already jogging towards her, staying well away from the water but remaining below the deep soft dry sand. He stopped before reaching Suzanne and stood with his hands on his hips, inhaling deep breaths of sea air and awaited her arrival.

"Good morning miss early riser. Did you walk from your home all the way to the beach? It must be several miles."

"Good morning Andrew. In fact, I ran most of the way. I needed some exercise and this beach has always been a good place to get some time by myself and just get away from it all."

Breathing more normally now Andrew smiled at Suzanne. "I hope 'it all' doesn't include me."

Suzanne reached out and took his hand in hers. "No, you silly boy. I meant the formal arrival dinner for you and my father – the surprise of seeing you – and all the visiting friends of the family, and I'm sure my mother is planning other events at the club. This stuff wears me out after a while and, I have to admit, I think it is all somewhat pretentious." Suzanne paused, looked down at the sand, shook her head and looked back up at Andrew. "I'm sorry. I guess that sounds horrible."

Andrew hesitated before speaking, looked warmly at Suzanne and finally said, "Well, now that you've said that, I fear I am the bearer of bad news."

With a resigned shake of her head Suzanne replied, "What now?"

"I have been sent to retrieve you – your mother knew exactly where you would be by the way – and remind you of the Ladies Luncheon at one o'clock at which your attendance, in full Ladies Luncheon attire I'm sure, is eagerly anticipated by all the ladies who have not seen you since you returned months ago. Oh, and you have an aunt from Toronto?"

Suzanne laughed. "Aunt Carol! The official black sheep of the family. She is my father's little sister who, at the age of seventeen ran off to Canada with a draft dodger. We never used to talk about her. I'm sure she is the reason I was sent away to an all girls' boarding school. Oh, now I have to run some more."

With that statement Suzanne let go of Andrew's hand and started running back towards her shoes. Andrew followed more slowly and when he arrived Suzanne was already sitting in the driver's seat with her shoes on.

"Did you actually drive my car all this way on the wrong side of the road? "

"I remained in the exact center and, fortunately, did not encounter another vehicle. I must admit, though, I did find it a bit distressing to shift with my right hand."

"A bit distressing? Andrew, one might suspect you are a bit British. If I may please have the keys, I will drive us safely home. Aunt Carol! I can't wait."

V

Andrew was sitting on the patio in a white wicker rocking chair, his feet on a wicker footstool, his back to the afternoon sun. Suzanne called to him as she emerged from the house. "So, here you are, reading the *Wall Street Journal*, studying for the real world."

Andrew quickly folded the newspaper and stood to greet her. "Well how was it? Was Aunt Carol as scandalous as you had anticipated?"

Rather than walking closer to Andrew, Suzanne turned away and walked to the far edge of the patio into the shade of the house. "It was actually quite horrid! Aunt Carol seemed as if she were trying to charm her way back into the family, even though my father is the one she should charm, and he of course wasn't there."

Andrew took a few steps towards her. "And this made it horrid?"

"Andrew, I don't want to be one of those people."

"Those people?"

"Those women, all dressed up, their hair and makeup perfect just to drink a glass of white wine, eat some salad, and make vacuous small talk while pretending they were enjoying it all. Aunt Carol couldn't even say anything interesting. She just smiled and agreed with whatever anyone else had to say."

"That sounds pleasant enough."

"Really? For whom? For me it was horrid. And I see my life too rapidly putting me right with them, smiling insipidly. Well, I can't do that!" With that statement Suzanne turned away from Andrew and went back into the house. A few minutes later, still standing, holding the now forgotten *Wall Street Journal*, Andrew heard the sound of Suzanne's car leaving the driveway, apparently in a hurry. He shrugged his shoulders and returned to the wicker chair.

Less than an hour later Andrew had completed his "study of the real world" when Suzanne again appeared on the patio.

"Ah, you have returned. Allow me to guess. You drove to the beach, sat on the seawall, and contemplated your future life."

"A not unreasonable guess, but alas, totally wrong. I went to the Dairy Queen and got a medium sized twist with sprinkles, which I then consumed, cone and all, sitting at a partially rusted round table under a faded umbrella."

Andrew stared at Suzanne a few moments before speaking. "Suzanne, all those words you just spoke were English, but I have no idea what they were meant to convey. I assume the Dairy Queen is not the winner of a bucolic beauty contest, but what is a medium sized twist, and what are sprinkles?"

"Andrew it's very simple. I did something fun, that's all. After that luncheon I needed something."

"Well, as your fiancé, I claim the right to ask of what this fun consisted."

"Granted, oh dominant male power in my life. Dairy Queen is an establishment that dispenses cheap soft-serve ice cream in two flavors, chocolate and vanilla. A twist is a combination of the two swirled into an edible cone. Sprinkles are small colorful sugar candies into which the ice cream cone may be dipped or rolled causing the sprinkles to stick to the ice cream. And, as a matter of interest, in Boston sprinkles are called jimmies. I have no idea why. You may consume your cone at one of their little outdoor tables or in your car, unless you care about the uphol-stery. The whole purpose is to have a sugar rush and a bit of fun."

Andrew paused, seeming to process this explanation and then spoke. "Clearly I did not offer to provide any fun when you returned from your horrid ordeal, for which I apologize." He then stepped closer to Suzanne and spoke softly. "Well we could sneak up to my room and …"

She cut him off. "No thanks. I'm going to take a shower and lie down. I need to rest and change my clothes for cocktail hour – another event from which I expect no fun."

Now, thoroughly confused, Andrew returned to the white wicker rocker, sat down, and wondered what it all meant.

VI

Suzanne's mother, wrapped in an old yellow afghan, was sitting at the glass topped patio table, holding a coffee cup and watching the yellow, brown, orange, and gold maple leaves add to the palette already starting to cover the bright green grass below. She greeted her daughter's arrival. "Good morning dear. That big sweater was a wise choice. It's starting to get chilly. I fear summer is really over."

Suzanne, carrying her own coffee mug, joined her mother at the table. "Those maple leaves are just beautiful. I saw you watching them fall." She sipped her coffee and continued watching the fall colors. "So, what exactly are Andrew and my father doing in New York this week?"

"I think your father calls it a 'meet and greet.' He wants to introduce Andrew to all the people in the New York office and some of their clients. He wants Andrew to be able to put a face with a name. And, of course, he wants to show off his soon to be son-in-law." She reached across the table and took hold of her daughter's left hand. "And while I'm on that subject I'm glad to see that you are wearing your ring more often. I was a little worried when you seemed to have put it away this summer. It really is quite beautiful."

Suzanne smiled at the ring. "I never wear it when I'm doing anything active, such as tennis or even golf. I guess I'm afraid of losing it or damaging it. Andrew told me it was some sort of family heirloom."

Her mother released her hand, sat back in her chair, and again watching the leaves fall said, "I don't suppose it had anything to do with Teddy?"

Suzanne sighed. "Of course it did. I didn't have it on the day he delivered the car because I had just come from playing tennis with you. Then, I was having so much fun I didn't want to scare him away. I know. I'm horrible. I guess I was just being selfish."

"Suzanne, being selfish isn't always a bad thing for a

woman. And I certainly don't think you are horrible. There was never any romantic involvement between you two was there?"

Suzanne drank from her mug before replying. "I don't know. He always treated me as some sort of princess, and he was my servant. But there were times when he would look at me and—" She paused. "I did have a lot of fun with him last summer and I feel horrible about the way he found out about Andrew. I had no idea that Andrew was the big surprise. I half expected another car. And then Teddy was so sweet to leave before I arrived so I wouldn't have to face him and try to explain Andrew."

They were both silent for a few moments. Her mother put down her cup. "Suzanne did you ever call him to apologize? You owe him that at least."

"No, I haven't talked to him since the day I invited him to the party. I told you. I'm horrible."

"No, you're not horrible. Why don't you call him and go have coffee together? You can apologize and tell him that you were enjoying his company and didn't want to make him uncomfortable about the fact that you were engaged."

"Really? Just like that?"

Her mother looked at her beautiful daughter, smiled at her, and said, "Yes dear, just like that."

VII

A crisp cool early autumn morning had now reverted into a slightly warm late summer day. The once dry air had softened and now held a pleasant caress of humidity. They were already on the second hole and neither had found much to say. Suzanne had apologized on the phone and Ted had graciously accepted. But now, neither knew what to say next. She was beginning to think that this golf date with Teddy had been a mistake. Could they really play even nine holes, each of them afraid to say the wrong thing? Her mother had probably been right when she had suggested just going for coffee. But to Suzanne, that had just felt too cold. And here she was now, silently watching Teddy tee-off.

Ted was confused as to what he was doing here. He and Suzanne had spent many hours together during the summer and then a week ago he had been told, by her father, that she was engaged to a person she had not once mentioned. Then yesterday a phone call, an apology, and an invitation to play golf. And when he asked if Andrew, the fiancé, would join them he was informed, "Oh, no. Just you and I." Was Suzanne still engaged? And where was Andrew? Ted wanted to ask many questions but decided to wait for Suzanne to start the conversation. It was she after all who had initiated this meeting. So far neither of them had said much. He pulled his driver from his golf bag, set the ball on a tee, and set his feet.

Ted swung and badly hooked his ball deep into the woods. He watched it go and then, not even thinking about it, softly said, "Whoopsie."

Suzanne's bright blue eyes opened wide as she turned to him. "Did you say just say 'Whoopsie?'

"I did. Sorry, not very dignified."

"Do you have any idea what Andrew would have said?"

"Not 'Whoopsie'?" Ted was almost laughing.

Now laughing herself Suzanne replied, "Teddy, you and I have to remain friends! Of course, I'll marry Andrew and all that, but I'm really going to need someone in my life who says

'Whoopsie' when he hits a bad shot."

Ted now looked more serious. "That's all I have to do? That's my one redeeming feature? Whoopsie?"

"Oh, I'm sure I'll find other equally difficult tasks for you. And no, you silly boy, that is not your only redeeming feature."

She retrieved a new golf ball from her pocket. "Here, try one of mine, they always go straight." And, as foretold, this time his drive was right down the middle of the fairway. Suzanne followed, also down the middle and ten yards beyond Ted's drive. Both feeling much happier and relaxed, they returned to their cart and proceeded down the fairway, this time easily chatting about nothing at all.

As they approached the fifth tee, still not having addressed anything of substance, they saw ahead of them a group of women who were moving slowly, talking loudly and clearly in no hurry. Ted asked, "Shall I get out and go ask if we can play around them?"

Suzanne smiled. "That's exactly what Andrew would have done, without asking me of course. No, this is a shady spot and we can wait." They both sat quietly, each wanting to talk but neither knowing where to begin. After a minute or so Suzanne turned to him. "Teddy, I apologize again for hiding the fact that I was engaged. It wasn't fair to you, but we were having such a pleasant time and I had no idea that Andrew would be the big surprise. I thought of us as good friends and I never even considered your thoughts. I'm really sorry if I misled you into thinking of me as more than just a friend. And I want to keep you as a friend — if that's possible. So, what can I tell you about Suzanne's other life?"

Ted hesitated and then spoke. "Well, if it isn't too rude, who the heck is Andrew and how did you meet him and how long have you been engaged?"

"Good questions indeed! God, I feel like such a rat. Okay, Andrew Whitaker is English, from one of those shires outside of London. Just as I was, he was sent to the finest boarding schools and then to university where he studied international business and finance. Can you see what's coming?"

"Noooo."

"Well, when Andrew finished his undergraduate degree, he was advised to seek an internship before proceeding with his graduate studies to make sure that was the career he really wanted. And of course, you know what's next."

"He ended up at your father's firm?"

"'Got it in one,' as the Brits like to say. So, my dear father molded Andrew in his own image. He designed Andrew's graduate program for him and stayed in contact with him on a regular basis. And then, during Andrew's second graduate studies year my father managed to introduce us. Now, I admit he didn't really say this but at the time what I heard was 'Suzanne, this is Andrew, the boy I have been grooming to be my son-in-law. I hope you like him.'" Ted's response was almost a laugh. "Really?"

"Probably not, but it felt that way. Andrew and I both felt totally embarrassed, but that actually brought us together. Of course, our parents made sure we spent the next year in constant proximity. And a year ago he asked me to marry him. So, that's Andrew and here we are. He's actually very nice, a little too serious sometimes, very smart, and I'm sure he will be a great success. But, Andrew has never in his life said 'Whoopsie' after making a mistake. Perhaps you could give him lessons."

Ted's response was simply, "I seriously doubt that could ever happen."

Ted felt he should say more but was again reminded of their two very different worlds. Would he and Suzanne even remain friends? Would she and Andrew move to Europe and out of his life forever? He decided to try to enjoy the rest of the day and see where it all went after that. The hen party ahead of them had cleared the green and Suzanne left the cart carrying her driver and walked to the lady's tees.

They caught up with the slow foursome at the next hole. Again, Suzanne suggested they just wait. It appeared that there was no one directly behind them. They sat quietly for a few moments and then Suzanne asked, "Would you like to hear about the wedding plans? Of course you would not, but I feel in the mood to vent so get comfortable. I'm so glad to have you to talk to."

"Okay, tell me all. I know nothing about wedding planning and am not at all eager to learn."

"Excellent! In the first place, I feel as if it's more my mother's wedding than mine. As soon as Andrew and I told our parents about our plans she flew into action. First, she checked availability of the big Episcopal church. The date had to be in the spring when all the flowering trees would be in bloom and the weather would be warm but not hot. Of course, I haven't been in that church since I was a little girl going to Sunday school, but I guess the churches are looking for paying customers. Once she had a few possible dates she went looking for the proper venue for the reception. This needed to offer indoor and outdoor accommodations and the outdoor spaces had to be beautifully landscaped. Of course, she was ready to re-landscape a place if that proved necessary. And then there was the search for the perfect caterer and a small jazz band—no noisy rock-and-roll nonsense for her daughter. Oh, did I mention the string quartet

ROBERT C. GWIN, III

for the church?"

By now the group ahead of them had moved on and Suzanne and Andrew resumed play. As they were following their drives Suzanne said, "And don't think I'm finished. I haven't yet described the great dress saga."

"I can't wait."

"It won't be long. Those ladies will stop again."

Trying to say something not too ridiculous, Ted asked, "So, you had to try on lots of wedding gowns until your mother approved?"

"Teddy, you have no clue." And with that she was on the green in three.

The next time they had to wait the cart was in full sun, so they left it and sat on a bench under the shade of the few leaves remaining on the tall oaks.

"Alright, here is the saga of Suzanne's wedding gown. First, forget all about something ready to wear. My mother knows a fashion designer who specializes in—what else?—wedding gowns, and who, for a hefty fee I'm sure, will design the perfect gown for the perfect bride. We had several interviews with this woman, who I really didn't like, and finally a 'sketching session' during which I was sketched wearing several of my own dresses and also just my underwear. Many measurements were taken and a month later two designs were presented to us. These were just designs, not the actual gown itself. Of course, my mother said to go ahead and stich up both designs and let's see how they look. This was done, a choice was made—I was not consulted—and final adjustments were made. When this was all completed my mother cheerfully informed me that if I gained any weight, fat, or muscle, she would have it surgically removed until the dress again fit perfectly. This entire endeavor probably cost enough to send me through law school for a dress I will wear for only a few hours one day in my life. And now I feel like whacking the hell out of a golf ball."

The fairway being clear, Suzanne teed-up and drove right down the middle to within twenty yards of the green. "There. I knew a little venting would improve my game!"

They holed out at the ninth green and Suzanne asked, "Had enough? We can stop here if you like."

"If you're sure you've told me all your worries and woes."

"Yes, the worries and woes of the very rich and very spoiled. How do you stand being around me?" Suzanne bagged her putter and asked, "So, who won, I assumed you were keeping score — Andrew insists on doing it."

"Not me."

"Oh well. Whoopsie!" They both laughed.

Even now in midafternoon, the cool dry air of autumn was returning to replace the warm moist air of earlier in the day. They rode back to the club, returned the cart, and walked together to where their cars were parked. Suzanne had to pick a few fallen leaves off the seat of her car and laughingly remarked, "Well, I guess this summer is finally over." She seated herself, started the engine, gave Ted a wave good-bye, and slowly drove away.

Ted picked a large oak leaf off his windshield and watched Suzanne depart. He murmured to no one, "Yes, I guess it really is."

ABOUT THE AUTHOR

Bob Gwin, known to his driver's license as Robert and to his family and close friends as Robin, grew up in Barrington, Rhode Island. Following high school, he considered studying writing at Rollins College in Florida, instead went to Swarthmore and Carnegie-Mellon and emerged as an engineer. Having retired from engineering, Bob has returned to writing.

For many years Bob was a member of Laughworks, a comedy Improv group that roamed the towns of Southeastern Connecticut searching for a permanent home.

Over the last four decades Bob has produced, directed and acted in community theater. He met Laurie, his wife of 36 years, at auditions for the classic "Chicken Every Sunday." They were both cast and have remained together ever since.

Bob and Laurie live in Gales Ferry, Connecticut, surrounded by trees, deer and an occasional fox. Bob's three children, Lauren, Rob and Caity have fled to the West Coast to avoid the New England winters.

www.ingramcontent.com/pod-product-compliance
Lightning Source LLC
Chambersburg PA
CBHW032004170626
46807CB00006B/2636